SEARCHING
IN THE
SYNTAX OF THINGS

SEARCHING

IN THE

SYNTAX OF THINGS

EXPERIMENTS IN THE STUDY OF RELIGION

Essays by MAURICE FRIEDMAN

T. PATRICK BURKE

SAMUEL LAEUCHLI

With an introduction by FRANKLIN H. LITTELL

FORTRESS PRESS   Philadelphia

Library of Congress Catalog Card Number 70–171494

ISBN 0–8006–0103–3

3028L71   Printed in the United States of America   1–103

CONTENTS

FRANKLIN H. LITTELL

INTRODUCTION

The time is right to bring out a book with experiments in the study of Religion. A heated national controversy is raging as to where, and where not, to do graduate religious studies. Intense debates are taking place about hermeneutics, phenomenology and philosophy of religion, and the role of the social sciences in the study of Religion. The problem of cross-disciplinary work is one of the most serious the universities face today. Three professors from the Department of Religion at Temple University are making their contributions to some of these issues in *Searching in the Syntax of Things.*

The study of Religion has expanded so rapidly in American colleges and universities that we are apt to forget how recently the discipline was added to the academic table of organization. The first major breakthrough came with the founding of the Department of Religion at Princeton University just before World War II. And in the state colleges and universities—with the single exception of the pioneer (1923) experiment at the University of Iowa—the remarkable expansion came after the *obiter dicta* of the U.S. Supreme Court in the *Abington* v. *Schempp* Case, 374 U.S. 203. The Court here approved teaching *about* religion, although it continued to outlaw liturgical exercises of religion from the schools. Dozens of universities moved to take advantage of the freedom of study, and in many of them today the most popular electives are in the new departments of Religion.

In earlier times, the study of Religion was embedded in the life and structures of separate religious communities. On that base, most of the work done was apologetic or dogmatic in nature. The new departments of Religion, however, find themselves in another setting. The modern university is overwhelmingly committed to the scientific (*techne*) dimension of knowledge: the analytical/critical/comparative/historical methods are featured, and advocacy—at least in religion!—is discouraged.

For several reasons this confronts the department of Religion with special problems, since neither students nor professors are generally ready to accept the intense departmentalization of advanced science as a given factor.

In the first place, we have enough evidence as to how people learn to know that some community of common purpose is essential. As Kurt Lewin, founder of social psychology, put it:

> *Acceptance of the new set of values and beliefs cannot usually be brought about item by item.*
>
> *The individual accepts the new system of values and beliefs by accepting belongingness to a group.*
>
> *The chances of re-education seem to be increased whenever a strong we-feeling is created.*[1]

Since the resources of a single religious community are no longer available to the department, at the very least a strong fellowship of teachers and students within the department is necessary. Even though the classical Platonic Academy was a religious fraternity (*thiasos*), and even though in the modern period we have had great learning centers in Indian *ashrams* and in communes like Esalen, the modern Western university does not allow the department to function as a "church." Moreover, the development of ecumenical cooperation within the Christian communities and of interfaith dialogue between the world religions makes such an effort retrogressive.

There is a second problem. The study of Religion should not be divorced from active concern for the actual condition of religious institutions and communities. We would not think much of a medical school which taught the history of medicine, the theory of health, and the philosophy of medical practice, without devoting attention to human persons both sick and well. If the problem of medicine today is that its devotion to *techne* has created an utterly nominalistic science, with both philosophers and general practitioners in short supply, Religion must have to do with man (and his religions).

The goal of Religion must remain, difficult as it is, to serve both science and wisdom. The university as a whole should do this, but there is overpowering evidence that the large modern university —with its specialized departmentalization—has largely lost sight

1. Kurt Lewin, *Resolving Social Conflicts*, ed. Dorwin L. Cartwright (New York: Harper & Bros., 1948), pp. 66–67.

of *man*. Many of the students who come to work in the Department of Religion do so precisely because they find there a surrogate for a true university.

The third and major problem is this: since the students and professors come from many different and rich traditions, where the prescientific and oral treasures are large, the first temptation is to repudiate the past and plunge into the demands of the present. The modern university encourages it. Science is contemporary and futuristic. But the Department of Religion, at least, must maintain the tension between what is received and what is analyzed, between what is remembered and what is freshly discovered. Kenneth Keniston has written of the personality type produced by the sheerly technical emphasis:

> The successful finished product of such an education is an individual who has the capacity to concentrate for long periods on assigned tasks, to remain cool, dispassionate, accurate, and objective to work, to undertake and carry through unaided complicated and long-range projects, to operate at high levels of abstraction, to work for long periods on tasks with no relevance to his everyday needs and experience.[2]

The qualities here described are much needed in the study of Religion. But "without vision the people perish." Moreover, without the dialectic the professor or student is apt to lose sight of his own time and place. As Reinhold Niebuhr wrote:

> The modern belief that "scientific objectivity" may be simply extended from the field of nature to the field of history obscures the unity of the self which acts, and is acted upon, in history. It also obscures the ambiguity of the human self; for the self as the creature of history is the same self which must be the creator of history.[3]

Good teaching develops the imagination as well as the fund of information. Good teaching increases self-awareness as well as

2. Kenneth Keniston, *The Uncommitted* (New York: Dell Publishing Co., 1965), p. 371.
3. Reinhold Niebuhr, *Faith and History* (New York: Charles Scribner's Sons, 1949), p. 12.

the capacity to produce products of sustained effort. Good teaching maintains the tension between openness to new insight and the necessity for closure and unity which our real life forces upon us in moments of decision.

Even study in the "hard" sciences involves participation. Recall the language of Francis Bacon:

> What he was asserting was two things at once: first, that the scientist must take the initiative, deciding for himself what he wants to know and this in his own mind in the shape of a question; and secondly, that he must find means of compelling nature to answer, devising tortures under which she can no longer hold her tongue. Here, in a brief epigram, Bacon laid once for all the true theory of experimental Science.[4]

The language of the rack may sound less than dialogical! But the principle is the same: whether in dialogue with the past or in discourse with those present, the study of Religion requires *Engagement*.

To preserve this quality of freedom, and to enliven the intellectual life of the human persons involved, the department encourages the use of many different idioms and methodologies. Communication to others is featured, as well as analysis. The essays here presented are chosen to represent some of the many options available, combining different methodologies and different structures of utterance.

The interplay of the rational and imaginative, of logic and magic, of the critical and the aesthetic, of *techne* and *logos* is basic to the study of Religion. Such interaction is required by the material itself, and it is also required by the peculiar historical situation in which the new academic discipline finds itself as surrogate for a true *universitas magistrorum ac scholarium*. With the modern university shattered into a thousand meaningless fragments, a veritable mirror of modern society's commitment to war and violence and divorce from the human measure, the study of Religion must walk a narrow path to avoid slipping into the swamp on either side.

4. R. G. Collingwood, *The Idea of History* (Oxford: Clarendon Press, 1946), p. 268.

For this reason my colleagues have dared to use the most varied methodologies to penetrate, define, and communicate some lessons from the study of Religion. The forms range from poetry to rationalism of classical type, but they have by no means exhausted the choice of methodologies available. Striking is the fact that all three essays point up the "layers" of human experience and analysis. For Friedman this means awareness of the attitude with which we meet each new experience. Laeuchli uses the term "hermeneutical consciousness." Burke emphasizes the personal and subjective nature of theology, and then calls upon the student to "step outside."

All of this underlines the necessary dialectic in any serious study of Religion, and it accents the freedom of a disciplinary dialogue which is still young and fresh enough to use many languages. The unique contribution of Religion in the university curriculum would be brought to an early death if that freedom, that tension, were sacrificed to a premature monism of methodology.[5]

The study of Religion, to which so many students and professors are now devoted, affords an opportunity to win out of chaos a new level of meaning. To that end, and to communicate it, the capacity for wonder is as essential as the capacity for critical analysis. The "hermeneutical spiral," which Ray Hart presented in his brilliant work, *Unfinished Man and the Imagination,* discloses the ground of freedom and creativity.[6] Doctors Friedman, Burke, and Laeuchli here explore in free and creative fashion some of the possibilities within that "spiral" as now available in the study of Religion.

The three authors represent a wide scope of background, training, and interest. Maurice Friedman, specialist on Martin Buber,

---

5. The intellectual and spiritual poverty of the "Welch Report" is chiefly evident in its nondialectical presuppositions, in its pendulum swing from repudiation of a former orthodoxy in religion to embrace uncritically the modern university's commitment to the machine and the value-system which serves it. The new discipline of Religion is thus pressed to leave old orthodoxies, which at least had the vitality of historic meanings, to serve the unreflective orthodoxy of mechanics! Claude Welch, *Graduate Education in Religion* (Missoula: University of Montana Press, 1971), passim.

6. Ray L. Hart, *Unfinished Man and the Imagination* (New York: Herder & Herder, 1968).

comes from the American Jewish tradition. His interests range from philosophy and religion to literature, psychology, and the image of man. Besides his teaching at Temple University he serves on the staff at Pendle Hill, a Quaker center in Wallingford, Pennsylvania. He has been actively involved in cross-disciplinary experiments at the university, the most recent being a carefully worked-out doctoral program in religion and psychology. He is well aware of commitment and witness as basic factors in religious studies, as he always has been in his writings on existentialism. But now he is concretely dealing with the interdisciplinary and inter-religious task. His idea of "touchstones of reality" lies at the center of his *via humana*, of his attempt to combine the awareness of relativism, in the midst of a pluralistic cosmos, with the conviction that we cannot live meaningfully in complete abandonment to subjective relativism.

T. Patrick Burke, Australian, Roman Catholic theologian with a Ph.D. from Munich, teaches Catholic theology and philosophy of religion. He has been widely involved in the contemporary debates in Roman Catholic studies and was the chief architect for the now famous St. Xavier Symposium in Chicago in 1964. His work seeks to answer the basic question posed by religious man: How am I to interpret life from the viewpoint of religion? If a particular religious statement were true, that Atman is Brahman, that Allah revealed the Koran to Mohammed, that Yahweh led the Jewish people out of Egypt, that Jesus of Nazareth rose from the dead, and so on, what difference would be gained by making such an assertion? What should it do to my interpretation of life? What light would it shed? What vision of things would be gained by making such an assertion? In a time of growing polarization in Roman Catholicism into conservative theology on one hand and radical, nonspeculative action on the other, Burke dares to raise radical questions about belief, and to talk in new ways about faith, hope, and vision.

Samuel Laeuchli, Swiss and Protestant, teaches patristics. His contribution in the book is twofold, a hermeneutic essay on Ignatius of Antioch and a poetic unit on "abraham and isaac." These two parts belong together, the first leading to the second, and Laeuchli uses both approaches in his teaching at the university. Caught in the dilemma between art and life, between intuitive creativity and intellectual analysis, he knows that he cannot have a fully consistent methodology. The word is ambiguous, life is ambiguous. What he can give, however, instead of a strict system, are stages, steps through which to find one's way, options by which to examine the object. Some of these examinations can be undertaken with a high degree of critical insight and lead to precise results, to the analysis of Ignatius of Antioch as a historical being. But at the same time, investigation includes response and hence belongs to one's evolution and to one's search. Precisely because Laeuchli is aware of this dilemma of the historian, and of the scholar altogether, he can be free to approach his field on another level, with poetic intuition, with his "logic of juxtaposition," a method reminiscent of the "absurd" in contemporary literature, a method which seems at first to ignore entirely the historical enterprise but which reveals at close reading that the poetry of replay yields insights which can be as profoundly "accurate" as those of the traditional academic enterprise.

Franklin H. Littell

Temple University
12/2/71

MAURICE FRIEDMAN

TOUCHSTONES OF REALITY
TOWARD A PHILOSOPHY AND METHODOLOGY OF RELIGION

"Alas the world is full of
enormous lights and mysteries,
but man hides them from him
with one small hand."
                    Baal-Shem-Tov

Touchstones of Reality*

The phrase "touchstones of reality" implies no separate and prior definition of "reality" or any metaphysical absolute. But neither can such touchstones be reduced to one or another form of subjectivism—whether it be the cultural relativist, the behaviorist psychologist, the Freudian psychoanalyst, the Sartrian existentialist, or the linguistic analyst. They offer no "reality" independent of themselves as "touchstones," but also no "touch" independent of contact with an otherness that transcends my own subjectivity even when I respond to it from that ground and know it only in my contact with it. A coloration that we take on from the culture or *Zeitgeist* but have not made our own is not a touchstone: it is only fool's gold. A touchstone cannot be passively received. It must be won by contending, by wrestling until dawn and not letting the nameless messenger go until he has blessed us by giving us a new name. Touchstones only come when we have fought our way through to where we are open to something really other than our accustomed set of values and our accustomed ways of looking at the world.

A touchstone of reality is either present to us or it has ceased to exist. However true our touchstone, it will cease to be true if we do not make it real again by testing it in each new situation. This testing is nothing more nor less than bringing our life-stance into the moment of present reality. In contrast to the scientist who is only interested in particulars insofar as they yield generalizations,

* In my book *Touchstones of Reality: Existential Trust and the Community of Peace* (New York: E. P. Dutton, 1972) I have developed a philosophy of existence the largest part of which grows out of my dialogue with the great religions and with problems of religion and ethics. In this present essay I attempt to extract and make more explicit the philosophy of religion and the approach to a methodology of religion which are implicit in this book.

we can derive valid insights from the unique situations in which we find ourselves without having to claim that they apply to all situations. We take these insights with us into other situations and test the limits of their validity.

Touchstones of reality are like insights, except that they are closer to events. An insight arises from a concrete encounter, but we tend to remove it too quickly and completely to a plane of abstractions. Any existential truth remains true only insofar as it is again and again tested in the stream of living. We have no secure purchase on truth above this stream. If we are going to walk on the road from touchstone to touchstone, we shall have to wrestle painfully with the problem of when it is right to move in the direction of insight and philosophical abstraction and when we must move back into the living waters.

As we move through life, our relation to the events of our past changes and with it our interpretation of their meaning. Sometimes these changing interpretations derive from new touchstones that we have acquired along the way. Sometimes it is the other way around: our new touchstones derive from our testing of the old ones and from our reinterpretation of the events of which they are the residue. This does not mean that we begin with raw experience and later add meaning or interpretation to it. We never have experience by itself. Our attitude toward experience is always present along with the experience itself, even at the moment we are having it. As we keep growing, however, our attitude changes—not only toward present experience but also toward the experience we have had in the past.

The very act of touching is already a transcending of the self in openness to the impact of something other than the self. When two people really touch each other as persons—whether physically or not—the touching is not merely a one-sided impact: it is a mutual revelation of life-stances. To communicate a touchstone is to witness. When we really witness, we hold the tension of the event out of which we witness *and* of the words, gestures, and actions through which we witness. We do not abstract what we have to say from the event in which it took root nor do we imagine that we can hand the event over as an objective fact minus the interpretation that we have made of it. For this same reason we have the right to ask that those to whom we witness do not limit themselves to the words that we use minus the person using them and what we are witnessing to in our own life. If we are making a witness, we are sharing something really unique with a unique person in a unique situation. Only in this way can we share our witnesses with one another. Because this sharing is real, it often happens that more than one witness, more than one touchstone is real to us at the same time. When this is so, we cannot exclude any voice, even when the voices seem to contradict each other.

Touchstones and Religion

My teacher Joachim Wach defined religion as a total response of the total being to what is experienced as ultimate reality. "Total response" because in religion, as distinct from scientific inquiry and aesthetic emotion, the whole being is responding and the whole being is involved in the response. Religion as we know it has always expressed itself in doctrinal forms as myth, creed, theology, metaphysics. It has expressed itself in practical forms as ritual, mass, and prayer—communal and individual. It has expressed itself in social forms as brotherhood, churches, and sects. It is impossible, indeed, to understand any actual religion except in terms of these expressions and their interrelation.

But for all that, one cannot reduce religion merely to these expressions and interrelations; for their matrix is the religious reality that is expressed, and what is expressed is not in itself directly expressible. One of the great errors in the approach of many people to religion is to see it as a form of philosophy or metaphysics which is going to prove that God exists or describe his nature and attributes. This is to reduce God to an object, a part of the universe, to make him subservient to our logic, and in any case has to do with the detached observer rather than with the involvement of one's total being. Religion is a way that one walks. Religion is a commitment. Religion is one's basic response whether or not he calls himself religious and whether or not he affirms the existence of God.

Nowhere is the approach of touchstones of reality more fruitful than in trying to understand religion. We do not comprehend religion if we imagine it to be a statement of creed or a feeling that rises within us or a theology or philosophy of religion that tells us about the nature and attributes of God. In entering into dialogue with the religions we are not looking for *the* truth, either in the sense of the Platonic truth—a metaphysical absolute—or in the sense of one religion's being true and the rest false, or in the sense of a "perennial philosophy" in which we can say what is the "essence" of all religions and what is only the "accidental," cultural expression. Insofar as we can enter into dialogue with a religion, each one will say something to us of its uniqueness and will say something to us about our life—our life as humankind but also as the particular persons that we are. Religion helps man understand himself because religions are, in the first instance, touchstones of reality. But these touchstones that have proved serviceable to other men can only become touchstones for us in real dialogue in which we respond from where we are. We cannot *become* Mohammed or Lao-tzu or the Buddha or Jesus, but we can meet them and know them in that meeting. We cannot be an ancient Greek, but we can respond with "pity and terror" to the downfall of Oedipus or feel in the depths of our own lives Socrates' drinking the cup of hemlock.

What is in common to all great religions is that each in its own way sees man as a problem to himself. Why is man a problem to himself? Because of the "given" of human existence. The awareness of self, of the passage of time, of change, in oneself, others, and the world, of the fact that one is mortal and will die, of the fact that one moves inexorably and irreversibly from youth to age, of possibility and the need for choice, or freedom and the checks on freedom by the limitation of our inner resources and the constraint of our natural and social environment, of one's dual existence in self-relationship and interpersonal relationship, in inner awareness and outer social role, of one's dual consciousness in waking and sleeping, in languor and intensity—all these in themselves make man's existence problematic for man. Through all of them there run discontinuities and confusions which force man to seek a reality amidst appearance, a stability amidst flux, an order amidst chaos, a meaning amidst paradoxes and incongruities. What is the self? What is time? What is reality? What is life and death? What is consciousness and what is the essence of the objective world? These questions have been an integral part of all human existence from the earliest times till today.

The Zen Buddhist asks, "When you are dead, and your body is cremated, and the ashes scattered, where are you?" "Then was not nonexistent nor existent," says the Hymn to Creation from the Rig-Veda, Hinduism's earliest scriptures, perhaps eighteen centuries before the Christian era. "Death was not then, nor was there ought immortal. . . . Who verily knows and who can here declare it, whence it was born and whence comes this creation? The gods are later than this world's production. . . . Whether he formed it all or did not form it, whose eye controls the world in highest heaven, he verily knows it, or perhaps he knows not." It is not such a long way from the Hindu concept of *maya*, the creative force that spins the veil of illusion—of time and place, name and form—to the deep pathos of verses that Vachel Lindsay wrote in his poem "The Chinese Nightingale" shortly before his suicide:

Years upon years I but half remember,
May and June and dead December,
Dead December and then again June,
Man is a torch, then ashes soon.
Life is a loom weaving illusion;
O who will end my dream's confusion!

Hinduism's special contribution to our understanding of the problem of man, the problem of the fully human, is its profound insight into consciousness, into subjectivity, into the relation of those to inner energy, motivation, and concentration, to the nature, the meaning, and the effectiveness of human action. The Hindu search for superconsciousness and for enlightenment raises the question of whether the essence of man, the true man, is to be found in consciousness or in the whole man, the whole person. Is it found by leaving the world that is given to us—the social world, the world of nature, the world of the senses? Or is it found by remaining in relation to the life of the senses and to other people? Is the goal of man enlightenment and individual spiritual salvation or is it a way of life which does not attain individual perfection yet affirms and redeems the human world? When inwardness and inner spiritual development are seen as the goal of life, external actions tend to become relative to the spiritual stage one has reached and the right way to act in terms of this spiritual stage. There is here an implied dualism not only between spirit and flesh, but also between individual consciousness and the social world which is considered, if not an evil world, at least a lesser world. This constitutes a great issue in the history of religions, one of those which exclude the possibility of any common "essence" that could be extracted from all religions. Does one relate to the world as a hindrance or a stepping-stone to inner perfection or does one believe that what is asked of one is a completion of the world which will forever leave oneself imperfect?

The history religions begin with the separateness and interrelation of God, world, and man. Revelation means for them that Transcendence enters into relation with the world—sets it free and remains in relation with it. It is not a question of whether God is a person, in the sense of being like a man. It is the question of whether reality is seen as a meeting with transcendent reality *within* which meeting nature and the cosmos arise, or whether it is the other way around: whether the cosmos becomes the all-inclusive reality in which man and God are set.

The Hindu notion of creation as "the play of the gods," or *lila,* has been rightly interpreted as "sitting lightly to the world," though this attitude only truly comes to those who have gone through and beyond the order and attained enlightenment. The history religions, in contrast—Judaism, Christianity, and Islam—speak not of divine sport, *lila,* but of divine destiny—in the sense that God himself has a stake in creation, in history. Instead of an event's being merely a part of a cycle or spiral, every event has its uniqueness and its own meaning. As Martin Buber puts it, "Meaning is open and accessible in the lived concrete." We do not have to put away the world of the senses, or nature, or time, or history to find this meaning.

Religious Symbolism and "Universal" Religion

We are confronted as no previous age has ever been with the variety of cultures and religions. We are in a position to distill the

essence from this variety, say many thinkers, and we owe it to ourselves and mankind to do so. In particular, there are many in our
age who claim to have rediscovered the secret of the mystics, who
offer us, in one form or another, keys with which to uncover their
hidden treasures of meaning. Seeing the essential unity in the
varied forms of religion, they quicken our hope for a universal
religion that will unite all generations and all cultures in a common brotherhood. Aldous Huxley, Gerald Heard, Ananda Cooma-
raswamy, Carl Jung, Henri Bergson, Erich Fromm, Bahai, the
Ramakrishna Society, the Ethical Culture Society—these are but a
few of the many thinkers and groups who have attempted to distill
out such a common essence.

The danger of these attempts lies in the failure of these thinkers
to understand the impossibility that their own formulations can
ever be universal religious essence divested of particular cultural
form. As a result, either they fall into a relativistic pansymbolism
which affirms all religious manifestations indiscriminately, or they
naively overlook the really important differences between religions and force them into a mold quite foreign to their spirit. As
soon as we say that this or that is the "essence" of all religions and
all the rest is only "manifestation," we are, of course, making a
selection. Every particular formulation of a universal religion
runs the danger of being an expression of a particular culture,
even when one is least aware of it.

The only way by which we can keep our foothold on the narrow
path between the forbidding cliff of a too rigid literalism and the
abyss of a too flexible symbolism is by an examination of the problems of religious symbolism. The symbolic is not a negation of
the literal but another and deeper level of reality. It is on the basis
of a careless, too easy, and one-sided interpretation of religious
symbols that many forms of occultism and universal religion
thrive, even as many religious sects keep their ranks by a too
literal, exclusivist, or traditionally distorted interpretation. Every
true symbol speaks to us in its own name, and yet it informs us
that it is merely a re-presentation of something beyond it. For
this reason we cannot entirely accept it as true or reject it as false.
The same applies to myth. Many myths contain a truth that we
cannot get in any other way. It is a dramatic capturing of truth in

an event rather than in a concept. But that does not mean that a myth is "literally true" any more than it is "literally false." A myth is a way of thinking, pointing, speaking which altogether eludes the criteria of "literalness"; nor can it be entirely captured within the category of the "symbolic," since it speaks out of events in time and involves the listener in the happening itself as many symbols do not.

The paradox of symbol interpretation lies in the fact that all symbols need to be interpreted and expanded, yet in this process much of the concrete reality that we held by the tight mesh of myth and symbol falls out of the frame of rational categories. The only fruitful course, then, is a dialectic between symbol and interpretation or, to speak more accurately, between one type of symbol and another—that of poetry and that of philosophy, that of religion and that of metaphysics, that of myth and that of concept —for, in matters relating to the transcendent, even the most literal and rational language can only be symbolic. Through religious symbols we experience the unconditioned as the boundary and source of everything conditioned, but the knowledge we attain of God through these symbols is not a theoretical, but an existential, truth, that is, a truth to which one must surrender in order to experience it.

The mystic claims to get beyond all symbols in direct contact with God, and the Hindu Vedantist claims that all religious traditions and all religious paths—those of devotion, discrimination, meditation, and action—lead to the same Absolute. But even the mystic and the Vedantist express themselves symbolically and mythically when they try to characterize what it is that they experience in their direct contact with the Divine. Aldous Huxley has called this mystical contact "unitive knowledge"—the union of subject and object in which one loses consciousness of one's self in the greater consciousness of the Divine. But if there is such union, it follows that when one returns to objective self-consciousness, one can find no literal or undistorted way of describing what one has experienced. Neither Huxley nor his philosophical counterpart, W. T. Stace, seems adequately aware of the difference between mystical experience and mystical philosophy or of the fact that experience can properly be interpreted in terms of quite different philosophies, each with equal metaphysical claim. Huxley and Stace assume, but in no way support, the nondualist mystical philosophy which they, unlike most mystics in the history of religions, hold to be the most valid interpretation of mystical experience. Since they would hardly claim to have reached the highest level themselves, what entitles them to judge which mystics have attained a "higher" stage of consciousness than others and which have come "nearer" to "God's self-realization"? Certainly not the testimonies of the mystics themselves; for they are by no means in agreement as to which experiences, symbols, and philosophies are the highest, nor can we divorce their statements from their immersion in particular cultures and religious traditions which lead them to interpret their mystical experiences in terms of one symbol or philosophy rather than another. The apparent tolerance of the modern Vedantist for all forms and manifestations of religion masks a value hierarchy in which the nondualist stands higher than the qualified nondualist, the yoga of discrimination than the yoga of action or worship, the impersonal Absolute than the God who can enter into personal relations with man.

There is a strong modern tendency to reduce religion to symbolism, in which the "symbol" no longer corresponds to a transcendent reality or derives from a meeting with the divine but is merely a manifestation of the psyche or an imaginative projection of man's own ideals and aspirations. "In earlier times, symbolism was regarded as a form of *religious thinking*," writes Abraham J. Heschel in *Man's Quest for God*. "In modern times religion is regarded as a *form of symbolic thinking*." This reversal of roles "regards religion as *a fiction*, useful to society or to man's personal well-being. Religion is, then, no longer a relationship of man to God but a relationship of man to the symbol of his highest ideals." No pragmatic "will to believe" can make such "symbols" believable. No psychological or social need to act "as if" these symbols had some reality independent of man can enable us to worship them.

Metaphysical analogies, as Dorothy Emmet has shown, are analogies between relationships rather than between one object which is familiar and known as it is in itself and one which is either abstract or unknown. To say "The Lord is my Shepherd" does not mean that the shepherd is a known, visible object corresponding to an unknown, invisible God. It means that my relationship to God, in one of its aspects, is analogous to the relationship of a good shepherd to his sheep (a shepherd such as we can imagine the young David to have been and not some modern employee of a slaughterhouse!). Heschel treats symbols in this active, relational way when he speaks of man as a symbol of God and interprets man's being created in the image of God as man's potentiality of becoming like God through imitating his mercy and love. "What is necessary is not *to have a symbol* but *to be a symbol*," writes Heschel. "In this spirit all objects and all actions are not symbols in themselves but ways and means of enhancing the living symbolism of man."

The symbol stands in twofold relation to the direct relationship that gives rise to it. As long as it is recognized as symbol, it may point back to the nonsymbolic religious reality. But when "the finger pointing at the moon is taken for the moon itself," as it says in a Zen Buddhist text, then it may stand in the way of man's meeting with God. The approach we have taken of touchstones of reality is less likely to fall into this danger than religious symbolism in general since the symbol all too often has static and visual connotations which easily lend themselves to false objectification.

This attitude toward religious symbolism implies a radical reversal of the idealist and mystical view which sees the symbol as the concrete manifestation of some universal, if not directly knowable, reality. The meaning of the symbol is found not in its universality but in the fact that it points to a concrete event which witnesses just as it is, in all is concreteness, transitoriness, and uniqueness, to the relation with the Absolute. The symbol does, of course, become abstract when it is detached from a concrete event. But this is a metamorphosis which deprives the symbol of its real meaning just by giving it the all-meaning of the "universal" and the "spiritual." This all-meaning is always only a substitute for the meaning apprehended in the concrete. Any symbol is, of course, itself a step toward the more general. If we speak of Adam and Eve and the myth of the Garden of Eden, this is certainly universal, but only in the sense that it happens with every man anew, not in the sense that it arises from something beyond space and time and concrete human existence. If we speak of the legend of the parting of the Red Sea, we are talking of a particular moment in history. As soon as we say that the Passover is a symbol of freedom, however, we have lost the immediacy of the historical moment—its uniqueness and concreteness—and have gone over into the realm of vague abstractions. Actually it is the other way around. Freedom is a symbol of the Passover. Freedom comes from that moment of history and others like it, and it becomes alive again in all concreteness in the Negro spiritual, "Go down, Moses," arising, as it does, out of the slavery of the black man in America.

We do not have to put aside particularity and the reality of time to find our touchstones of reality. On the contrary, they have to do with the full seriousness of the moment. The fact that this moment will not come again does not mean it is an unreal or illusory moment. It is the only moment that is given us now to make real. When the symbol means the covenant between the Absolute and the concrete, its meaning is not independent of lived human life in all its concreteness. Not only does this lived concreteness originally produce the symbol, but only this can renew its meaning for those who have inherited it and save it from becoming merely spiritual and not truly existential. William Blake bases his poem-preface to "Milton" on the historical fact of Jesus walking in Jerusalem: "And did those feet in ancient time," but he transposes the setting immediately to contemporary England: "Walk upon England's mountains green?" And he ends by demanding that that ancient event be real in the present, "Among these dark Satanic Mills":

> I will not cease from Mental Fight,
> Nor shall my Sword sleep in my hand
> Till we have built Jerusalem
> In England's green & pleasant Land.

"All symbols are ever in danger of becoming spiritual and not binding images," writes Buber. "Only through the man who devotes himself is the original power saved for further present existence." Buber does not mean the man who devotes himself to the symbol the way a theologian might. He means the man who devotes himself to the hour, who involves his whole being in his response to its claim. The life of such a man, his nonsymbolic meeting with the people and things that confront him, may ultimately, indeed, be the truest and most meaningful symbol of our relation to the divine. The highest manifestation of the religious symbol is a human life lived in relation to the Absolute, and this relationship is possible even when there is neither image nor symbol of God but only the address which we perceive and the demand to which we respond in our meeting with the everyday. In an age in which our alternatives seem increasingly to be reality divested of symbols or symbols divested of reality, the prerequisite to an image of God may be the rediscovery in our lives of an image of man: an image of authentic human existence.

Rather than develop an objective theory of hermeneutics, such as Joachim Wach did in his book on "Understanding" (*Das Verstehen*), I prefer to come to understand less precisely and more relationally by way of touchstones of reality. Starting with touchstones, we can understand the unique relationship of the person or group to the event. We can also understand the problem of the renewal of touchstones in future events and the problem of communication and handing down of touchstones. Last and perhaps most important of all, we can understand the problem of the "dialogue of touchstones." My answer to the dilemma of religious particularism versus religious universalism is the mutually confirming pluralism of touchstones of reality. Religious witnesses are renewed when a situation or event speaks so powerfully that a John Woolman can suddenly hear in the American wilderness the teaching of George Fox, not as a doctrine to be preached but in his whole life—in his relations to the Indians and the black slaves, and his fellow Quakers.

The enormous importance of touchstones of reality as an approach is that such an approach does not claim to be the absolute truth, but it also does not abandon us to some completely subjective relativism. It witnesses to as much reality as we can witness to at that moment. In opposition to both the *via negativa* and the *via positiva*, I would make bold to call touchstones of reality the *via humana*. Only through it can we keep close to the concrete reality, without pursuing theology at the expense of the fully human or humanism at the expense of closing man off from the nameless reality that he meets in his meeting with everyday life.

Man does not have to have a "religion" to exist as man, but he does have to have basic trust, he does have to have touchstones of reality. I do not believe any man lives without some sort of touchstone of reality, but a great many people do live without formal religion. Anyone who says that these people do not have ethical concerns or spiritual qualities is mistaken. I am more concerned with basic attitudes than belief, with religious reality than with religion. Every religion perhaps originates in and points to religious reality, but it also often obstructs it. Even the community in which we meet and confirm one another at times also obstructs the immediacy from which our touchstones spring and to which they have the power to point back.

Religion and Psychology

A great deal has been written about the psychology *of* religion, but very little has been written about psychology *and* religion. As long as we think in terms of psychology *of* religion, then psychology is given license to dispose of whatever in religion falls, or seems to fall, within its jurisdiction. Whatever does not is conveniently referred to some other discipline. But as soon as we think in terms of psychology *and* religion, then a meeting is envisaged on equal terms between two essentially different realities: a body of knowledge within the structure of a science and a body of tradition, ritual, history, and experience accessible in parts to many sciences and as a whole to none. To envisage this meeting is to raise a question which is almost by definition never raised within the field of psychology *of* religion, namely, the limits of the psyche as a touchstone of reality. "Psyche" here is used in the most general sense possible—mind and soul, conscious and unconscious, thought, feeling, intuition, and sensation.

Today the psychological in the sense of objective analysis and the psychic in the sense of subjective experience are confusedly intermingled. Yet this confused intermingling has taken shape in the popular mind not only as a single phenomenon but as *the* modern touchstone of reality in the way theology was for the Middle Ages, physics for the Newtonian age and the age of Enlightenment, and evolution for the mid-nineteenth to the mid-twentieth centuries. Here I am using the phrase "touchstone of reality" in a derivative, objectified, and cultural sense rather than in an existential sense, that is, as a product of some direct encounter with an otherness that transcends our own subjectivity even when we respond to it from that ground. These two senses of "touchstones of reality" are often distinct but seldom entirely so since we live in culture and our contacts with any reality whatever are refracted through culture—including language, concepts, world views, ways of seeing, thinking, and experiencing, attitudes and expectations.

But if there is no contact with reality which is wholly separate from culture, there *is* culture which is far, far removed from any direct contact with reality. In this latter case our "touchstones" become both obstacle to and substitute for any immediacy of apprehension or reapprehension of the reality known in mutual contact. The limits of the psyche as touchstone of reality is a problem for this very reason. For those who take the psychological or the psyche on faith as ultimate reality, the question of touchstones of reality in the more immediate and concrete sense in which they derive from concrete encounters or events can hardly arise.

Carl G. Jung, in contrast to Freud, is open to every variety and manifestation of religion. So far from considering religion an illusion, as Freud does, Jung finds in the religions of mankind the golden ore which, when it is extracted and refined, becomes the alchemist's stone not only of healing but of personal integration and spiritual fulfillment.

Yet the collective unconscious, or objective psyche, is a more basic and all-inclusive reality to Jung than God. God too is a "psychic reality like the unconscious," an archetype that already has its place in that part of the psyche which is preexistent to consciousness. Our problem is thus transformed from the limits of the psyche as touchstone of reality to the limits of a psychologism which tends to swallow up all other reality. "Not only does the psyche exist, it is existence itself," writes Jung in *Psychology and Religion: East and West*. He defines religious experience, by the same token, "as that kind of experience which is accorded the highest value, no matter what its contents may be," and by value he means psychic value. The only action that Jung recognizes as real is from the unconscious and never from any independently other person or reality. Hence he states, "God acts out of the unconscious of man." "It is only through the psyche that we can establish that God acts upon us," and, "Only that which acts upon me do I recognize as real and actual." God is indistinguishable from the unconscious or more exactly from the archetype of the Self within the unconscious.*

Once when I was teaching the biblical prophets in a college class, I was startled by a freshman who insisted that Isaiah was a paranoiac. "How can you call him a paranoiac?" I asked. "A paranoiac is one who lives in a sealed-off world of his own whereas Isaiah was more aware of the realities of history than any man of his time." "Well then," the freshman replied, "he was an educated paranoiac!" While few of us would express ourselves with such frankness and naiveté, most of us are really on the student's side, even if we are not aware of it. If any of us had Isaiah's vision in the Temple, we would be more likely to consult a psychiatrist then to exclaim, "Holy! Holy! Holy!" Though we are far beyond Freud's dogmatic and simply negative approach to religion, popular Freudianism still dominates our thoughts and provides our most tenacious cultural "touchstone of reality." The search for linked causes, the distrust of motives, one's own and others, the distrust of the conscious, the conceptual, and the "merely verbal," the loss of trust in the immediacy of our feelings, intuitions, and insights, the loss of trust in our own good faith and that of others, enclose us round in a well-nigh hermetically sealed psychic ecology.

If the psyche is not given to us as an object that we can analyze, dissect, or even interpret according to the universal hermeneutic of myths, folklore, and fairy tales, neither is it given to us as sheer immediacy. Not only is it never accessible to us from without or in abstraction from a living person in relationship with other persons and with nature, but also we never experience it directly minus an attitude toward it, a personal stance which already constitutes

* For a treatment of Jung's psychology of religion, see my essay "Religion and Psychology: The Limits of the Psyche as Touchstone of Reality," *Quaker Religious Thought* 12, no. 1 (Winter, 1970), and for my discussion of Jung's total thought, *To Deny Our Nothingness: Contemporary Images of Man* (New York: Delta Books, 1968), chapter 9.

an interpretation of it. The attempt to identify the psyche and truth—never more boldly made than by Jung in his universals of meaning originating in the psychic depths—must always shipwreck on the fact that truth means a relationship to *existence*. It can never be restricted to one aspect of existence—the inner to which all the outer must *de facto* if not *de jure* be subordinated. Like the nineteenth century theory of social harmony arising from laissez-faire in which each follows his individual interests, this necessitates a magical assumption of one universal which guides us separately in such a way that all is somehow for the best together. Either truth is reduced to the psychic and becomes mere tautology or the psychic is elevated to Truth and becomes a false hypostatizing.

None of this is to deny the overwhelming experience which we all have at some time or other of a revelation that comes to us through the psyche, whether it be dreams, intuitions, or the liberation and expression of emotions so deeply suppressed that we did not even suspect their existence. But this is revelation precisely because the psyche is thus brought into the fullness of human existence and interhuman coexistence, not because the truth already exists as such "down there" in the psychic depths or "in there" in the hidden recesses of our being.

Religion and Literature

The collector's urge of modern man leads him to seek a universal myth in the myths of all peoples, whether it be that of the flood, of creation, or of the dragon and the dragonslayer. These myths were man's first way of thinking—dramatic events rather than discursive reasoning. We try instead to derive a secondary meaning by identifying resemblances among myths. We extract a perennial myth and feel we are very close to the heart of reality when in fact we are freezing on the doorstep. No myth catches us up as it did ancient man so that for that moment all that is real and important is the heightened reality of the mythic event. The mythmonger asks us to accept a rich sense of everything having significant relation to everything else in place of any immediate insight into any particular event or reality.

Both the symbolmonger and the mythmonger tend to see particular literary works as endlessly reproducing universal themes and in so doing lose the very heart of religion, literature, and myth. They find the meaning of literature in the static symbol or concept and not in the concrete unique event and its dramatic, dynamic unfolding in time. A similar distortion is introduced by those who reduce a work to a single point of view—*Moby Dick* as "Melville's quarrel with God" or Billy Budd as a Christ symbol—or who identify the author's conscious intention with the intention that is implicit in the book. Dostoyevsky wrote a letter to his niece in which he said, "I want Prince Myshkin to be a Christ figure, a really good man, a Don Quixote." But the intention that becomes manifest in *The Idiot* is very different from this conscious intention; for Prince Myshkin is not in the least like Christ. He does not say to the woman caught in adultery, "Go and sin no more," but seeks instead to marry her and destroys both her and himself in the process. The Thomas à Becket whom T. S. Eliot presents in the first act of *Murder in the Cathedral* as a complex man, tempted by motives of pride to be lowest on earth in order to be highest in heaven, cannot be dramatically squared with the predestined martyr, the "Blessed Thomas," of the second act.

The very effort of the more sophisticated to avoid the mismeetings between religion and literature often leads to another, equally serious mismeeting. That is the attempt to preserve the separateness of theology and literature as disciplines, languages, or modes of consciousness while searching for a metatheory that underlies them or a formal meeting after each has attained a reflective distance from the literature itself. Whether this metatheory takes the form of a philosophy of symbolism, a phenomenology of linguistic comprehensions, a psychology of unconscious archetypes, or an ontology of the disclosure of the meaning of being, it has the same effect of relating religion and literature in terms of concepts and world views rather than in terms of the work itself. If religion and literature are not already united in the piece of literature before us, no aesthetic or theory of symbolism will bring about their meeting.

Some seek to avoid all mismeetings by restricting the intercourse between religion and literature to an examination of literature for its explicitly religious contents. Comparing literary expressions of doctrines, cults, and social groupings is valuable, of course. But still more valuable is comparing the basic attitudes toward reality reflected in literary images of man. This is so only if religion is primarily understood neither as an objective philosophy nor as a subjective experience but as a lived reality which is ontologically prior to its expression in creed, ritual, and group. At the same time, it is inseparable from these expressions and cannot be distilled out and objectified in itself. The religious at this deepest level might be described as a basic *attitude* or relationship arising in the encounter with the whole reality directly given to one in one's existence. From this standpoint, many works of literature are as close to religious reality as any work of theology, for both may be products of some genuine religious encounter. This approach means taking seriously the full address of literature to the wholeness of man. The most fruitful approach to the meeting of religion and literature, therefore, is not to treat literature as if it were covert theology but to discover in our meeting with it that image of authentic human existence that is implicit in the very style of most great literature.

The image of man, understood as a basic attitude toward reality, is a ground that is not identifiable in the first instance as literature, theology, religion, or philosophy though having implications for all of them. Religion and literature do not meet in the once- or twice-remove of theology and literary criticism but in a matrix deeper and older than both of them. If we go back behind the time of the rise of a secular literature, generally seen as a worldly distraction to be kept away from young girls and from the religious, we find that originally literature was one of the basic expressions of numinous awe or wonder, as in the Vedic hymns and the Psalms. The Book of Job was not "the Bible as living literature"; it was living literature that was later taken into the Bible. When I first began to teach in college, I was struck by the fact that because the Book of Job was in the Bible, my students regarded it as an expression of blind faith and were blocked from understanding the actual text. They read it through the eyes of what their ministers called "faith" but what was actually no more than a mind-set, toward which their elders were positive and they negative.

The meeting of religion and literature is not achieved by starting with the finished ideas of religion and then trying to find literature to illustrate them. We must, rather, dig deeper into both religion and literature in order that we may recover and discover for ourselves that ground where they are one: those basic human attitudes which arise in our response to ultimate life-realities and to the daily life-situations that confront us. The notion that so many people have today that meaning in literature is to be found most directly in the novel of ideas or the drama of ideas is exactly backwards. On the contrary, we only reach the level of abstraction and timeless ideas after hundreds of thousand of years of dealing with the more concrete in legend and in myth. Even drama began as a religious celebration; only much later did it acquire fixed roles and parts and become the detached drama of our stage. Religion and literature have a common matrix, and that matrix still informs their meeting when it takes place. Literature, indeed, is often far closer to original religious reality than any of its later objectifications in creed, doctrine, theology, and metaphysics.

It is only personal involvement combined with obedient listening and faithful response to the voice of the other that addresses us in the novel, poem, or play that enables us to take literature, "religious" or "secular," out of the brackets of the purely aesthetic or the merely didactic so that our own image of man, or basic attitude, may enter into dialogue with the image of man, or basic attitude, underlying the work that confronts us. If religion means bringing the whole of one's existence into dialogue with the "nameless Meeter," then literature as genuine personal dialogue must be an integral part of religious reality as we know it. Religion and literature, then, would not be thought of as different modes or languages, however much theology and literary criticism may be properly spoken of in that way, but as differing degrees of fullness of a single dialogical reality. If this means in one sense subsuming our dialogue with literature under our meeting with ultimate reality, it means in a still deeper sense that our meeting with ultimate reality takes place only within the very structures and events of our concrete daily existence, no unimportant part of which is our dialogue with literature.

It is in the problem of point of view more than any other that the metaphysical dimension of Herman Melville's great novel *Moby Dick* is to be found. This metaphysical dimension is not the picture of what reality *is,* but of man's relation to that reality. The changing, ever-shifting point of view in *Moby Dick* corresponds with the ever-changing, ever-shifting attitude of man toward the reality that confronts him. *Moby Dick* is a gigantic poem in which each stanza, each image, is of significance in itself, and which at the same time moves along from image to image and from chapter to chapter in such a way that the meaning of each particular image must be found within the dynamic, dramatic progression of the whole. *Moby Dick* is a metaphysical novel, but we must distinguish between the explicitly metaphysical passages which Melville so liberally strews throughout for poetic and symbolic purposes and the implicit metaphysics which we touch on only when we have gone through the dramatic situation and the characters into the basic attitude toward existence that we glean from the interplay of symbolic suggestion, action, and point of view.*

Touchstones, Trust, and Truth

With no sure ground under his feet, contemporary man seeks for touchstones of reality around which to center his experience, structure his values, guide his life. If he is open to his full potentiality, he finds not one but several touchstones. At times the iron filings of his life are pulled in different directions by magnets each of which claims to be *the* touchstone of reality. One of the most important double pulls experienced by the open man is that between the exploration of "inner space" through mystic meditation and the call to make real the space *between* man and man in the life of dialogue. This is not a question of "inner" versus "outer" since the interhuman, when it is genuine, demands that the inwardness and uniqueness of each partner be brought into the meeting. But it is a basic decision as to priorities. Is "all real living" higher or expanded consciousness or is it "meeting"?

To say that we can have some contact with reality without having to make the claim that it is *the* reality, to say that we can have touchstones of reality and even share them—that takes a certain trust along the way. Touchstones of reality are not uni-

* The above section derives from a projected section of my forthcoming book *The Hidden Image of Man* under the chapter title, "Literature and Religion: Meeting or Mismeeting?" For my interpretation of *Moby Dick* see *Problematic Rebel: Melville, Dostoievsky, Kafka, Camus,* 2nd ed. rev. (Chicago: The University of Chicago Press, 1970).

versal ideals shining above history and above our own lives. They are existential realities that remain meaningful only insofar as they are shared, witnessed for, and made living again in the present. We do not need to use the same words as others or even to affirm that beneath our different words and images we really mean the same thing. In contrast to those who proclaim a perennial philosophy, we can accept the fact that we not only have different paths but that these paths may lead to different places. What matters is that in listening to the other we hear something genuine to which we can respond. We receive from each other without ever being identical with each other; we are able to affirm and respond to what we receive, and grow through it. The oneness of God, to me at least, is the renewed meeting with the ever unique and ever particular. It is not some type of superabstraction above time and space.

The reality of pluralism must be the starting point of any serious modern faith. We should give up looking for the one true religion and consider our religious commitments as unique relationships to a truth which we cannot possess. We should also give up the notion that some men possess the spirit and others do not. The spirit that speaks through us is a response to the spirit that we meet in others, the spirit that meets us in the "between." The spirit does not stand in contrast to words. I finds its true life in the encounter of words when that encounter means caring and concern, in the contending of words when that contending means witnessing and confirming. Going *through* the word to a meeting *beyond* the word can be a more powerful witness to the imageless God than any dogma, creed, theology, or metaphysics.

"God-talk" is objective; "experience-talk," whether mystical or simply religious, is subjective: "I have had these feelings or this experience." Touchstones of reality point toward something which is neither objective nor subjective. For that reason they have a great deal to do with the way we walk in our daily lives but very little to do with the way we *think* about this walking, since our thinking usually remains bound up with the objective and the subjective.

In our search for meaning, for touchstones of reality, we sometimes confuse two quite different things—a comprehensive world view that gives us a sense of security and the meaning that arises moment by moment through our meeting with a reality that we cannot embrace. Many people when they have a religious or mystical experience move quickly to a metaphysics and identify their experience with one particular philosophy of religion or of mysticism. Not content with having found meaning in immediacy, they want to wrap up reality in some conceptual totality and use their experience as the guarantor of that totality. Perhaps one of the most important witnesses that can be made in our day is that it is not necessary to have a *Weltanschauung*, a comprehensive world view, in order to be able to live as a man. What is more, our "world view" may get in the way of our confrontation with the concrete at any given point and just thereby rob us of the real world. This means, in terms of theology, that our stance, our life-attitude, is more basic than the affirmation or nonaffirmation of a "Being" or "ground of being." No intellectual construction, not even the philosophy of dialogue, can ever include the real otherness of the other. In meeting the other, I come up against something absurd in the root meaning of the term—something irreducible that I cannot get my arms around or register in my categories. If this is true of the otherness of every concrete other, it is true by the same token of God.

A world view is like a geodesic dome. It creates a special atmosphere for you, keeps certain air currents up, and gives you a sense of spaciousness without giving you the real world where the winds blow freely and sometimes uncomfortably. A world view exists within your consciousness, even when you share it with any number of other men. No matter how adequate the world view is, it leaves out otherness by definition. For that is the very nature of the other—that it cracks and destroys every *Weltanschauung*, that it does not fit into any ensemble of coherences, that it is absurd. You can fit others into your world view, but you cannot do so without robbing them of what makes them really other.

There are two different meanings of the word "ground" as we use it in a phrase such as the "ground of being." One of these is found in conceptual, or ontological, formulations. The other is a ground only in the sense of what we can touch on in our situation, in our experience, in our existence—what gives us the courage to take a step forward and then perhaps another step forward and still another. With the former meaning of "ground" I can have nothing to do because it presupposes getting behind or above creation. This desire for a comprehensive gnosis may give satisfaction to our minds when we give in to it, but we cannot live our lives from there. It goes beyond the given of our existence, of our finite freedom and our finite-infinite knowing. The other meaning of "ground" I can and do affirm, for this is precisely what I mean by "touchstones of reality." Existential trust has to do with this second meaning, but not necessarily and often not at all with the first. Existential trust does not depend upon a man affirming that he believes in God or that he has faith in God. What a man believes, in the conscious, rational sense of that term, often has little or even a negative connection with his basic life-attitude, his stance.

What does this say about God? Abraham Heschel says, "God is of no importance unless he is of supreme importance." That means that a "God" who is just a means to our ends is not really God. Jean-Paul Sartre says, "Even if God did exist, that would change nothing." In contrast to both Heschel and Sartre, the vast mass of men want to keep God around for his usefulness—for the national welfare, for successful living, for positive thinking, for peace of mind or peace of soul. In the face of this situation, the truly religious man, or in our terms the man who is deeply concerned with touchstones of reality, must sometimes, like Albert Camus, have the courage to put the belief in God aside in order to try to make contact once again with existential reality. "I want to live only with what I can know," says Camus. I want to find touchstones of reality that I can live by. In our age this man in his "atheism" may affirm reality more than those who profess the existence of God.

We meet the "eternal Thou" only in our existence as persons, only in our meeting with the other: we cannot know it as if from outside this existence. If we recognize this, we must renounce the attempt to include God in any conceptual system, even the most creative and organic of process philosophies. To say that one meets God in what transcends oneself does not mean that the other one meets is "supernatural," or even that the "supernatural" is in the "between." The term "natural," however, leads us to forget the reality over against us and to see our existence as entirely included in a conceptual totality which we call "nature," "world," or "universe." In our actual experience, reality, including all other selves, is not only within but over against us. It is not some common, undifferentiated reality that can be seen from the outside. Much modern thought confuses the subjectivity of the person and the subjectivity of "man": it treats man as a totality and what is immanent in him as if it were in a single self. In our concrete existence, however, there is no such totality. The Thou confronts us with the unexpected, takes us unawares. We must stand our ground yet be prepared to go forth again and again to meet we know not what. It is not insight into process but trust in existence that enables us to enter into a genuine meeting with the unique reality that accosts us in each new moment.

To speak of "touchstones of reality" does not imply that we can define what we mean by "reality." All we can say is that we mean the concrete situation, including whatever enters into it from all that we have been. There is a relation between our various truths—our touchstones of reality—both those that we experience in our own lives and those that we encounter in the lives of others. But this relation is not one of an abstract consistency. We cannot stand back and look at those events from which we derive our touchstones as if in the moment of reflection we were outside of time. Rather in a new situation it is possible to reaffirm the old touchstones—not in such a way as to say that they are the same as the new, but they are illuminated by them. If this leaves us with no absolute or truth other than the relation to the moment, into that relation may enter every other truth-relationship that we have made our own. We do not *have* truth. We have a relationship to it. We can affirm certain moments of meeting—not necessarily as having an objectifiable knowledge content but still as not being sheer immersion in the flux. These moment by moment truth-relationships do not yield some higher truth that we can objectify as always the same. All we have is what at any given time we know *and* what we are not given to know. The notion that man is moving toward omniscience, that science will some day know everything there is to know, simply misunderstands the fact that all human knowing is a mixture of finitude and the infinite. All our knowing is partial ignorance. What we should be concerned about is what it is given us to know at *this* time. In each new discovery or rediscovery our earlier touchstones of reality are brought into the fullness of the present. Any reference point beyond that would take us out of the only dimension in which we live and think and know—the dimension of time. We must, of course, act as if we were above time when employing our useful abstractions—from mathematics and logic to engineering and even some parts of law. But in the essential matters of our lives, in our concrete existence as whole persons, we must avoid the illusion that we can rise to a reference point above existence itself—an abstract spatiality divorced from events.

If I meet my friend again, I can recognize him, know him again, only if there really is a new relationship. Otherwise I remember him from our past moments of relationship, but he has not come alive to me again as my friend. If I do recognize him in new relationship, then the old has been given new meaning through being brought into the new without destroying its original meaning. Similarly the God that I *re*-cognize, that I know again, I know in concrete uniqueness, not in any abstract sameness. Objectivizing, structuring, formulating are essential in the carrying forward of our truths. But if we content ourselves with them alone, we lose our touchstones of reality. We have to take the further step of bringing the old touchstones into the new. Therefore, our ultimate criterion of meaning and truth is not the objectification of a structure but the lived new meeting with reality.

For this reason we cannot find touchstones of reality by going back to tradition. We can only find them through renewing tradition, through making it living again in the present. I believe, with St. Augustine, that we live in the present alone—that the past is memory, the future anticipation. In Deuteronomy we read, "Not our fathers, but we here, the living, stand on Mount Sinai to receive the Covenant." This does not mean that there is no difference or tension between our fathers and us. "Over an abyss of sixteen hundred years I speak to you," says St. Nicholas at the beginning of Benjamin Britten's *St. Nicholas Cantata*. We are aware he is speaking to us, but we are also aware he is speaking to us across an abyss of many centuries. If we attempt to "continue" tradition without the awareness of this abyss, we lose the tension. If cutting off from tradition is one danger, there is an equal danger in retaining the time-hallowed symbols yet reading into them new meaning so freely that, like Peter Pan's shadow, it becomes tacked on to the old. Only when we have three elements—our personal uniqueness, the will to be open, and holding the tension with tradition—is there a meaningful dynamic. We must fight and contend with tradition in order to make an honest witness to our own uniqueness and to all the absurdity and incongruity that has entered into our lives.

"From wonder into wonder existence opens," says Lao-tzu. To have a touchstone and to touch touchstones means a whole different way of living than is implied by locating the reality "out there" or "in here." Many of us feel that if we only replace the anthropomorphic notion of God with some impersonal concept, we are on the way. But what are we on the way to except another abstraction, unless it lead to greater openness? The only "perennial philosophy" I can espouse is that each of the religions and touchstones that I have entered into dialogue with points toward greater openness. "Alas the world is full of enormous lights and mysteries," says the Baal-Shem-Tov, "but man hides them from him with one small hand."

T. PATRICK BURKE

THEOLOGY AS PART OF THE
STUDY OF THE PHENOMENON OF RELIGION

> "But the Solar System!" I protested.
> "What the deuce is it to me?" he
> interrupted impatiently: "You say that
> we go round the sun. If we went around
> the moon it would not make a pennyworth
> of difference to me."
> Arthur Conan Doyle, *A Study in Scarlet*

Somewhere around the Mediterranean, about the time of the reign of the Roman emperor Domitian, a man writing an account of the doings of some religious zealots penned the sentence, "Jesus is Lord." Today, in the United States of America, I, heir of that group of zealots, product of centuries of culture fashioned by their outlandish beliefs and their amazingly enduring organization, yet living in a world so different from theirs that it might be another planet, ask myself what I am to make of that assertion of theirs, "Jesus is Lord." How can I understand it? What does it mean? What does it say to me?

This essay is devoted to the thesis that from now on theological questions can be usefully asked only within the framework of the study of the general phenomenon of religion. That is, the traditional doctrinal convictions of, say, Christianity can be adequately understood only if they are seen in the first instance as religious assertions of the same species as Hindu, Buddhist or native African religious assertions, and are analyzed and interpreted in light of the way in which religious assertions *in general* function. It will be maintained that religious assertions function characteristically as expressions of a vision of life, and that, therefore, the chief task of theology is to uncover the details of the particular vision of life which is in question. The theological question about a religious assertion is: If that were so, what difference would it make to my interpretation of life?

I

Theology takes as its starting point assertions which have come to constitute a religious tradition. They are, in the first place, inherited, not invented. But we do justice to any tradition, religious or otherwise, only when we view it from the outside as well as from the inside. The full reality of a culture, for example, is not disclosed to someone who knows it only from within. The German who knows only Germany does not know Germany. The American who knows only America does not know America. Similarly the Jew only has a just understanding of his own religion when he has some idea of how it appears to the non-Jew. The Christian sees Christianity rightly only when he takes into account the way a non-Christian sees it.

One of the first things the view from the outside brings to light is that one's religious tradition, like other traditions, does not have an "essence." Books have been written with the title, "The Essence of Christianity." But it is not possible to say of any historical movement that it has an essence, and this holds true of Christianity as well. Therefore, it cannot be the task of theology to disclose this essence. Like any other tradition that exists in history, a religious tradition is a bundle of strands, coming together here and separating there. Where some lines come together, we put a string around them, as it were, and tie on a label so that we can talk about different aspects of the bundle more easily. When we are dealing with a religious tradition, the view from the outside tells us that we are not dealing with simple continuity, or a straightforward and essential unity, but with discontinuity and with multiplicity—a bundle.

However, there are places where this multiplicity comes to a focus. Objectively, the various strands that make up the tradition come to a focus in documents accepted as authoritative, such as the sacred scriptures of the religion, creeds, or official doctrinal statements. These constitute an objectification of the tradition, and it is these normally which theology takes as its point of departure.

Subjectively, the tradition comes to a focus in the individual person. It is in the mind of the individual, in his conviction, his understanding of life, that the tradition lives and has force. The only religious faith that actually exists is the faith of the unique individual.

Therefore the only theology possible is one that elucidates the faith of the individual. It is not possible to have a theology that reproduces "the Christian faith." A theology is always the theology of one man. It represents his unique belief, developed against the background of his unique experience of life. Its function can never be to relieve others of the task of grappling themselves with the issues involved. It must act as a stimulus to them to develop their own conception of the religious tradition, that is, of the meaning of human life, insofar as this is possible.

Talk about "theology" is difficult because the word is deceptive. People, including theologians, frequently have the impression that there is one thing that goes by this name, and the only methodological task is to state what it is, the true "essence" of theology. So, for example, we find conferences on "the relation between philosophy and theology," as if each of these words stood for a single thing. But the most diverse and varied activities are carried on under these names. The principal thing that distinguishes schools of philosophy is not their convictions about things, but their convictions about the function of philosophy: Is it to analyze human existence (e.g., Heidegger), or the operation of language (Wittgenstein), or the concepts of other sciences (Carnap), or the character of experience (Hume, the positivists and pragmatists); and if this last, does this include the experience of consciousness (Husserl) ; or is the task of philosophy to improve the philosopher (Plato, Spinoza)? Battles between schools of philosophers appear to have arisen largely because each wished to claim that what he was engaged in was the sole legitimate task of "philosophy."

In the same way, the word "theology" covers a multitude of enterprises. I can attempt to defend a belief I was taught in childhood. I can defend official doctrinal statements; I can try to reformulate traditional beliefs in new conceptions; I can try to deduce one belief from another by logic. I can try to solve the problems that a fellow believer has with our tradition, or that an unbeliever has. I can try to answer questions that the tradition raises, or I can try to answer questions that experience raises about the tradition. I can also ask: What difference would a particular belief make to my vision of human life?

There is no point in trying to decide which of these is "theology" and which is not. All are possible. What we have to decide is which of them, if any, is the most useful thing to do here and now.

At another time and place some other undertaking may be more beneficial.

II

An assertion is a statement of alleged fact. The facts asserted by religions are of two very different kinds. Some are matters of history, events which it is believed have taken place in the past, or will take place at some time in the future, such as the exodus of the Jews, the resurrection of Jesus, or the general resurrection of mankind from the dead. Others assert metaphysical facts, such as that there exists one God, or one God in three persons, or that Atman is identical with Brahman and multiplicity is an illusion. Although we do not commonly refer to assertions like these as "facts," still a religious tradition considers them to be so, that is, actually existing, objective states of affairs, true in themselves, quite apart from whether they have any effect on the individual. In this sense, religious convictions are considered to be convictions about the most important of facts.

There is a distinction between the form or appearance of a statement and its function.

We can make a statement for the primary purpose of pointing out an objective matter of fact, without any suggestion that the fact makes a significant difference to us personally. These may be called "factitive" statements.

By contrast, we can make a statement for the purpose of indicating a significant difference which we believe is made to us by some state of affairs. These may be called "importative" statements, that is, statements expressing importance, or, in a special sense, "meaning." (The noun "meaning" will be used exclusively in this special sense here, to avoid confusion.) To designate the specific content of an importative statement, the (Old English) noun "importancy" may be used, if it does not seem too cumbersome. It is possible for a statement to have the form or appearance of a factitive statement, and yet function as an importative one.

When I speak of "factitive" statements, I am not implying that the statement is true, or even that it could possibly be true, but only that the person making it is not making it primarily to express a significant alteration in his own condition.

Two women are out window-shopping, and one, pointing to a

dress that had looked green from a distance, remarks, "This dress is blue." It is a detached observation, made out of curiosity, and she passes on, her personal situation unaffected.

But suppose she is going to be bridesmaid at a wedding and she has ordered a yellow dress from Christian Dior for the occasion because the color suits her hair and complements what the bride is wearing. When it arrives and she opens the box, with its $2500 price tag, she utters the sentence, "This dress is blue." Although the verbal formulation of the statement is the same, its function is notably different. In the second case numerous substitutes are imaginable which would scarcely occur in the first. She is not making a detached observation out of curiosity; she is expressing a significant difference she believes is made to her own condition. The utterance has the form or appearance of a factitive statement, but it functions as an importative one.

While scientific and philosophical statements mostly belong in the first group, that is, are factitive in character, religious statements belong in the second: even though they may have the appearance of stating facts, as in doctrinal assertions, prayers, etc., nevertheless they function as statements of importancy, or "meaning" in the sense mentioned. Statements like "There exists a Supreme Being," or "Moses led the Hebrew people out of Egypt," taken as the factitive assertions they appear to be, are not religious statements at all. Taken as they stand, the first is a metaphysical assertion, the second a historical one. They become religious only when they function as importative statements.

The evidence for this thesis, if evidence is needed, is not hard to find. What reason does a religious person, as distinct from a historian or philosopher, have for asserting such things as that there exists a Supreme Being, that the inmost soul is identical with Brahman, that God revealed the Koran to Mohammed? It is not curiosity, historical or metaphysical, that moves him. It is a conviction that in some way his own condition is personally affected. This alone is the source of his interest in them. So there exists, or does not exist, a Supreme Being. So what? What difference does that make to me? Unless the Supreme Being in question is of such a kind that my personal situation would be affected by him, I may have a metaphysical curiosity about him in odd moments, but I have no religious interest. The God of the deists is not capable of being an object of religious concern.

It is a particularly interesting feature of importancies that different facts can yield the same importancy, "make the same difference." To come back to the bridesmaid with the blue dress: it is actually a matter of complete indifference to her that the dress is precisely blue. It might just as well be pink or purple, as long as it is not the color she wanted. A green dress with red spots would make exactly the same difference to her as the blue one. Within a certain spectrum, to be discussed later, the facts may change considerably, yet have the same importance. It may be a matter for argument whether a man died from hypertension or hypoglycemia; as far as the man himself is concerned, the difference is the same. He is dead.

The religions of mankind have a remarkable power to adjust their factitive beliefs. Christians long believed it to be a matter of religious faith that the world was made in six days. When this was discovered to be scientifically unlikely, it was decided that "day" in Hebrew (*yom*) could mean a very long time, rather than twenty-four hours. Finally the biblical account was interpreted as a poetic rendering of the general "fact" of creation.

If we were to ask an adherent of the Jewish faith about the exodus of the Hebrew people from Egypt under Moses, he would be likely to assert that this historical fact was of great importance to him. But suppose we were able to put before him good historical evidence that the event known as the exodus actually took place over a number of years, in different groups of people, so that Moses could be the leader of only one of them, what will his reaction be? Will he give up his religion? It is possible; but it is more likely that he will say: The fact remains that God revealed the Law to Moses, and that is what counts. If we carried the argument further, and we could prove that the figure of Moses was a later creation, say of the ninth century B.C.E., to provide a historical focus of unity for the Hebrew tribes, will he now give up his religion? Again, possibly; but more likely he will declare: Well, I know what it means to be a Jew, and for me the Jewish religion bears within itself the marks of a divine origin; if you wish to say that the story of Moses is a poetic expression of this reality, that's all right. The divine sanction of his religion is maintained, and that is what matters to him. He has thus preserved the importancy, the meaning of his religion to his own satisfaction. But he has come a long way in his factitive beliefs.

Statements can make different sorts of differences. A difference can be made to my physical, financial, or mental state. We need to ask more closely: What sort of difference is made in my condition by a religious statement?

In appropriate circumstances, "This dress is blue" translates into "I am angry." It expresses an alteration in an emotional condition. The statement is emotionally significant. This was the sort of significance which the logical positivists, such as A. J. Ayer, attributed to religious statements. The assertion "God is good" is expressive of a feeling of happiness or contentment, for example.

Or an assertion may express an intention to act in a certain way. If someone says to me, "Let's rob the corner bank tomorrow," and I reply, "That's a good idea," my response, though in form an assertion of value with regard to his mental activity, need not be a detached observation, but may express a momentous decision to undertake a rapid and only slightly hazardous means of acquiring wealth. If the action decided on is being looked at from the viewpoint of its morality, then the statement is "ethically significant." Following Braithwaite, many analytic philosophers consider that this is the way religious statements function. The statement "God is love" is equivalent to "I intend to act in a loving way."

But it is also possible for the difference to be of a cognitive character, that is, to lie in a *perception* regarding the condition of the speaker. The statement, "Mr. Nixon was elected President of the United States," uttered by a historian or reporter, has the form, and perhaps the function, of a factitive assertion. Uttered by Mr. Humphrey it might be presumed to express primarily a perception concerning his own condition.

Since this type of statement expresses not an emotion, not an intention to act in a certain way, but a perception, the question arises: What sort of perception?

The significance of the question, "What difference does it make?" was first stressed in philosophy by Charles Sanders Peirce, the founder of American pragmatism. Peirce suggested it be used as a tool to obtain clarity in metaphysical statements and as a criterion to judge them. But, as observed, there are different sorts of differences, and the sort of difference Peirce was looking for is very different from the one that applies in the matter of religion. The difference Peirce and William James required is one in the realm of sense-perception. For a metaphysical assertion to be worth making, there must be some way in which our sense-experience would be different if the assertion were not true: for example, the type of experience we have when we attempt to verify a theory in physics or chemistry by seeing something through a microscope or on a measuring instrument. This also seems to be what Braith-waite demands when he says that for religious assertions to be cognitively significant, they would have to make some observable difference to our experience.

But in addition to sense-perception in the ordinary use of the term, where we see, hear, touch, taste, or smell something, there is another type of perception that consists in seeing a pattern in things where we had not seen one before, although the observable sense-experience remains the same. For example, I look at a lot of dots on a sheet of paper, and after ten minutes I suddenly see a face there. Or I am walking along a country road and I see a stick on the ground, and my companion says to me, "That is a snake," and then I *see* that it looks like a snake. A similar type of perception is at work when a psychologist looks at the observable phenomena of human behavior and sees in them a pattern corresponding to Freud's theories, while another, looking at exactly the same activities, sees a pattern that corresponds to behavioristic theory. The question whether such a type of perception can be validated or verified, how it can be assessed, is another matter. For the moment, it may suffice to point out this type of perception and to suggest that it is within this realm that religious statements belong, as importative statements of a perceptional character.

The religious man then sees something differently. What does he see? I think we must say that he sees life differently. That is to say, it is not a question of seeing an isolated event in a different light; it is a matter of how he interprets his overall experience. It is, in some sense, the totality of his life-experience, taken precisely as a totality, which is interpreted.

If Jesus of Nazareth was God, then our interpretation of human life must change. We cannot justifiably go on doing business as usual. If the Koran was revealed by God to Mohammed, then we need to rethink our overall approach to things, not just to this or that. If our impression that we exist as distinct individuals is an illusion, then our conception of what life as a whole is all about must be altered. The interpretation which we place on the totality of experience is at stake in these things. A religion presents us with a vision of life.

Phrases like "a vision of life" or "the meaning of life" are notoriously vague. It would be helpful if we could arrive at a clearer notion of what it is we are talking about. It would be especially helpful if we could discover the elements that make up such a thing. If we are going to talk usefully about "visions of life," we need a fairly strict conceptual framework which will enable us to deal with them with some intellectual rigor, so that we can effectively compare and contrast them, for example. The following schema is proposed as only one of what might be numerous possibilities.

1. In the first place, there is a statement, explicit or implied, about the principal *problem* man faces in life. What is the chief obstacle to human hope? Usually there will be an assertion that some particular aspect of experience constitutes our main difficulty.

It is possible, for example, to experience the world of nature as the principal problem of life. In primitive cultures and religions this tends to be an unreflected assumption, where human existence is obviously dependent on the grass, the sheep and cattle, the crops, the sun shining and the rain falling at the proper time. In Chinese thinking, nature has been grasped explicitly and profoundly as the source of man's existence, and the framework of his life. In the reflective Taoism of the *Tao-te Ching* and Chuang Tzu it is man's lack of harmony with nature that is responsible for his woes. Man is not the measure of nature, he is part of it, and is to be understood in terms of it—nature is the measure of man. If nature is supreme, to be out of harmony with it is disaster. This is man's chief problem in life, and the experience of it is the main obstacle to hope.

(This conception of man's chief difficulty in life is not confined to Taoism, as might seem; it also applies to Confucianism. The Confucian concern with the right ordering of society, and even the neo-Confucian concentration on "the moral mind," exists within an overarching framework that sees society itself as part of nature. Not that Confucianism developed the "romantic" attitude to nature that characterizes the Taoist poets, but it develops within a characteristically Chinese conception of man and society that sees both in terms of what is possible within the given framework of nature. If Chuang Tzu and the *Tao-te Ching* deal explicitly with the problem of how to live in harmony with nature, the Confucian tradition deals with the problem of social structures; but social structures themselves are experienced as a problem precisely insofar as they are not a deliberate creation of man's, but are part of the intractable soil of our lives which we call "nature.")

Another conception of man's chief problem in life is that it lies in the experience of suffering as such, that is to say, not in nature but in man himself—that part of man which suffers, the suffering self. It is this conviction that lies at the roots of the religions of Indian origin, Buddhism and Hinduism. What would you do if you found yourself in the middle of the Sahara with a toothache? That is perhaps not too far from the problem which both religions deal with. The Buddha expressed it clearly: the whole of life is suffering; "birth is painful, old age is painful, sickness is painful, death is painful, sorrow, lamentation, dejection, and despair are painful." The Brahmanist Svetasvatara Upanishad utters the same insight:

> Forgetting his oneness with thee,
> Bewildered by his weakness,
> Full of sorrow is man.

To be a human being is necessarily and inevitably to suffer. I am my own worst enemy. Not nature—nature would have no power to hurt me if I did not let it. It is I who allow it to overwhelm me, who give it its power over me. Both for Brahmanism and Buddhism, man's principal problem is himself, his distinct, individual existence, which lays him open and makes him vulnerable to the painfulness and restrictions of finitude.

Another possible conception of man's principal problem in life, and a very different one from the preceding, is that it consists in my fellowman, more accurately in my relationships with my fellowmen. In this case the chief obstacle to hope is not nature, nor myself, but you, that is, my relationship with you. Here man is not viewed as a part of nature, but as a person who stands uniquely against nature and in contrast to it. The distinctive notion of personhood is highly developed. Correspondingly, man's outstanding hindrance in life is the experience of sheer nastiness, the hardheartedness of human beings toward each other. Acute awareness of injustice lies at the root of the ethical religions, and their most fundamental conviction is that justice must be done some day. This view characterizes the Semitic religions, Judaism, Christianity, and Islam, and also Zoroastrianism. Since it is in this realm that ethical notions, in the stricter sense of the term, apply, these religions have developed ethical and moral conceptions, such as sin, conscience, and repentance, much more fully than the Chinese or Indian. (Reference to Confucianism as primarily an ethic is only justifiable if the word "ethic" is understood in the most general sense, as referring to a pattern of desirable activity.)

This one problem, of the relationships between people, can be experienced in a variety of ways, depending largely on the prevailing stage of cultural development.

In the primitive society of nomads and agriculturists-with-difficulty of ancient Persia, the problem posed itself in the simple terms of "the good" versus "the wicked," the "war of the sons of light against the sons of darkness," to adopt a later but appropriate title. When a certain degree of sophistication has been achieved, this naive dualism is at least partly overcome, and the possibility can be considered that "wickedness" may be present in me too and not only in the "enemy."

In the tribal society of Israel, the problem presented itself in terms of tribal relationships with the rest of mankind. The period of development of classic biblical Judaism, after 538 B.C., is marked by the ambiguity of the necessity of ethnic unity as a condition of survival and restoration, on the one hand, and, on the other hand, the exilic and postexilic experience of the larger world beyond, the unity of the Persian world empire, and later of the Graeco-Roman world. Judaism has never escaped from this tension: it has never been simply a tribal religion, but it has also never been able to become simply universal in scope. Its experience of the problem of relationships between people has consequently been marked by the same tension; relationships with mankind in general are important, but relationships within the ethnic group have a special importance.

The step to a fully universal scope in the religions of Semitic origin was made with Christianity, and subsequently followed in Islam. In both cases, the problem which the religion is designed to tackle is that of the relationships between people in general. However, the religion's ability to deal with the problem is conditional on people's joining the religion, so that, on the one hand, there is a consciousness of the special importance of relationships between members of the religion, and, on the other, there is a drive to incorporate the whole of mankind within the religion. Even so, the problem of interpersonal relationships which Christianity is designed to deal with is not identical with that of Islam, since Islam's emphasis on the fulfillment of a law flows from a concern for the public aspect of the problem, while Christianity's attachment to an individual savior-figure identified with a historical person is an expression of a greater emphasis on private relationships between individuals.

Another possible conception of man's principal problem in life is that it consists in the repressive and exploitative character of social structures. This is the conviction with which Marxism begins. Although social structures are entirely created by people, once created they tend to take on a life of their own, and they then act back on the people sustaining them, remolding and refashioning their creators. Men are the prisoners of situations of which they themselves are the authors. It may be that this problem is felt as an economic one, as in classical Marxism, the division of society into exploiters and exploited; or it may be experienced more as an existential problem, the fact that my identity as a person is created by the people around me, rather than by myself; or it may be viewed primarily as a case of social repression in terms of general power rather than of class economics alone, as seems to be the case with the "New Left."

In any of these cases, the attitude of individual people to one another, whether good or bad, is not the problem. It is irrelevant whether a person is "well-intentioned" or not. The decisive thing is the role he acts out in society, the function he performs. If he is, in fact, a member of an exploiting or repressive class, no amount of "goodwill" can rectify the situation. He must either change his public activities or else run the risk of elimination.

Another conception of man's principal problem is that it lies in the absurdity of life. This view has been expressed with impressive force, especially since the Second World War by such writers as Sartre, Camus, and Beckett. Life is meaningless and futile, non-sensical, preposterous, and monstrous. This conviction is not the product of a set of reasonings; it is an experience, an experience which renders hope ridiculous. According to this conviction, religious systems which offer man hope blind him to the reality of life, and deprive him of the limited pleasure he might have had a chance to enjoy.

In the actual course of life, unreflected upon, no doubt all of these things mentioned—nature, suffering, interpersonal relationships, the repressive character of social structures, and sheer absurdity—and others as well are experienced all together, in a vague and undistinguished way, as constituting the obstacle to human hope. People do not often settle on one particular issue as "the principal problem." But it is proper to speak of an *interpretation* of life only when the elements of experience are distinguished, priorities assigned, and the vision structured.

How do you decide what does, in fact, constitute man's principal problem in life, if there should be such a thing?

It seems likely that no one principal problem would be valid forever. What is experienced as the chief obstacle to hope will probably vary with the cultural situation, that is, from culture to culture, and within the one culture as it develops from less to more advanced forms. As a culture becomes more sophisticated, so do its problems. To experience distinctly the repressive character of social structures—especially in a psychological way, as creative of personal identity—as the principal problem in life, already requires a relatively advanced level of civilization; it is a rich man's disease.

2. The second component that we find in interpretations of life is some sort of proposal about an *ideal solution* to man's principal problem in life. There is not necessarily any logical connection between the solution and the problem, but some state of affairs is suggested as providing a remedy for the chief of man's ills.

If the problem is man's lack of harmony with nature, it is natural enough to decide that the most desirable state of affairs would be one in which man achieved harmony with nature. This is the ideal proposed to us in the *Tao-te Ching*. Harmony with nature means fitting in with nature, not trying to impose one's own desires on it, not treating it with violence, but allowing it to give expression to itself. "The weakest things in the world can overmatch the strongest things in the world." "The world cannot be shaped; nor can it be insisted upon. He who shapes it, damages it; he who insists upon it, loses it." The wise man "lets all things develop in their natural way." If a man wishes to remain straight, he must be prepared to bend; it is when he resists rigidly that he is most likely to be broken.

The Way of nature is beyond man's grasping. To attempt to encompass it in concepts is self-defeating: "When all in the world understand beauty to be beautiful, then 'ugliness' exists. When all understand goodness to be good, then 'evil' exists. Therefore he who knows does not speak; he who speaks does not know."

If man's principal problem, on the other hand, is the experience of suffering, one conceivable remedy would be to disengage, if possible, that portion of the self which suffers. This would mean an inner rearrangement, an interior adjustment of the mind, so that the suffering is no longer experienced, and therefore ceases to be suffering. If this could be achieved, it would solve the problem of pain in general, whereas attempts to remove the external cause of pain, for example by the use of medicine, will only work from case to case, and a new remedy has to be discovered for each occasion. The latter is the way of science and technology, to proceed piece by piece, trying to overcome one individual problem after another. The former, the way of interior mental adjustment, is the solution offered by the religions of Buddhism and Hinduism, each in its own way.

Early Buddhism was clear and explicit that it was offering this remedy. In the Buddha's *Sermon at Benares,* after it has been stated that the experience of suffering is man's chief problem in life, and that the cause of suffering lies within man himself, in his inordinate desires, "the craving for passion, the craving for existence, the craving for non-existence," we are told that the remedy lies in detaching oneself from oneself, so that the portion of the self which suffers is let go and disengaged.

> Now this, monks, is the noble truth of the cessation of pain, the cessation without a remainder of craving, the abandonment, forsaking, release, non-attachment.

While Buddhism treats the problem directly on the practical level, and deliberately abstains from metaphysical speculations, Hinduism in its early reflective stage, as represented in the Upanishads, and later in the Vedanta schools, deals with the problem by putting forward a profound, highly abstract, mystical, metaphysical system: the doctrine that all things are one, that multiplicity is an illusion, that at the core of its being every entity is identical with every other entity, and thus there exists only one real being, hidden from us now by the veil of our senses. Suffering belongs to the world of experience, which is an illusion. It is overcome when we realize our fundamental unity with the One. This One, Brahman, is identical with the true Self of every human being. It is immortal, not subject to suffering and death. Therefore, our search is a search for our true Self, which lies beyond all death and pain.

> Brahman alone is—nothing else is.
>
> He dwells deep within the heart. He is the Lord of
>   time, past and future.
>
> Having attained him, one fears no more,
>   he is the immortal Self.
>
> > Katha Upanishad

If man's principal problem in life is conceived to be his relationships with other human beings, then it is natural that the ideal remedy for his condition will be seen in a state of affairs where ethical wickedness is overcome and men treat one another properly. Where sufficient sophistication has been reached to perceive that ethical wickedness is just as likely to be present in myself as in others, the removal of past failures, that is, the forgiveness of sin, will be a prerequisite.

This condition of things, where sins have been forgiven, and men treat one another rightly, may be designated as "ethical salvation." It is described in Zoroastrian literature as "the House of Song," in the New Testament as "the Reign of God," and in the Koran as "paradise." Although these images of "heaven" frequently give a first appearance of being simply a place or state of happiness, closer examination shows them to have strongly moral features. These religions look forward to the triumph of moral goodness over moral evil. They are animated by the conviction that justice must be done one day. The "House of Song" represents the victory of the good over the wicked, who are assigned to the "House of the Lie." When the "Reign of God" is described, it is in terms of the attitudes of people toward one another, as in Matthew 25. The Muslim "paradise," although pictured in very physical terms, is for those who "give sustenance to the poor man, the orphan, and the captive." It is for "the righteous" who "dread the far-spread terrors of Judgment Day," while "for the wrongdoers He has prepared a grievous punishment" (Surah 76).

(It can be suggested that the ideas of a personal God, of a judgment, and of a "Reign of God" to come, naturally lead a religion to emphasize personal ethics, and no doubt that is possible. The suggestion being made here, however, is that, from the viewpoint of the way these religions function in the lives of people, the reverse is the case. It is the strongly personal experience of evil, that is, of evil as a matter of the attitude of persons toward another, of the "good" versus the "wicked," that expresses itself in the ideas of a personal God, a judgment, and a "Kingdom of God." When the naive notion is overcome that it is possible to divide mankind into "the good" on the one hand and "the wicked" on the other (an event rarer in practice than in theory), when, for example, the conviction grows that both of these elements are to be found mixed in all people, and no clear-cut ethical separation of mankind is possible, or that human behavior is more a matter of psychology than ethics, then the ethical religions are in danger.)

The details of the conception of ethical salvation vary some-what, but the essential idea is present in each case. Sometimes it is expected to occur within history, as its final and crowning epoch, as in late Jewish and early Christian apocalypticism, or, in a much more refined version, in the work of Teilhard de Chardin. Some-times it is located outside of history, e.g., the Koranic paradise. Sometimes the two notions are combined, as in the Christian doctrine of heaven and the day of judgment.

Where man's principal problem is identified as the repressive character of social structures, it is natural that the ideal remedy will be constituted by a state of affairs where social structures are no longer repressive, whether economically, psychologically, or politically, according to the more precise definition of the prob-lem. The classless society of Marxism, the ever-renewed revolution of Mao, and the ideal of the rural commune in the United States are instances of this type of solution.

If man's principal problem is felt to be the experience of the absurdity of life, one possible remedy for this, at least a means of dealing with the problem, is the ideal of having the strength to acknowledge the absurdity and not flinch before it, to "stick it out" and refuse to lose heart, though realizing that hope is vain. (Whether this can be considered an "interpretation" of life is perhaps open to question. It is a reaction to life, an attitude to-ward it. But an interpretation would probably be a perception, or a claim to perception, of a pattern in some sense intelligible, which is here rejected by definition.)

3. The third major component of an interpretation of life con-sists in a statement about the *realization* of the ideal solution. This component seems to contain two chief elements.

a) One element is an estimate of the *chances* of the solution being realized. It may be that the ideal solution remains an ideal, as in Confucianism, which never nourished high hopes that the Golden Age of Yao and Shun would return. Or it may be that it is up to us whether the solution is attained or not; it is possible, but there is no guarantee. This would be true in general of Buddhism. Or it may be that there is a guarantee, an assurance, that one day the ideal solution will actually come about. This is the case with the Semitic religions' expectation of "the Reign of God," and Marxism's classless society. This element, the degree of certainty with which final realization of the ideal is expected, is crucial for any interpretation of life. It makes a vast difference whether human life has a purpose, a goal, built into it, that is, whether it already exists toward an ultimate realization, or whether in itself it is purposeless. In the first case life has "meaning" of itself; in the second case it is we who must give "meaning" to it by setting up our own goals. In the first case the notion of "importance" and so the notion of "value" and of the value of my life have a cosmic scale of reference, one beyond myself, and one that must therefore be respected by other people. In the second case, the notions of importance and value are derived from the individual, and my life has value essentially only to myself, because it belongs to me, although it may acquire value for other people for reasons such as love or need for help. If it is expected with assurance that the ideal state of affairs will one day be realized, then the first of these options is implied: life has a goal built into it. If final realization of the ideal state of things is not expected with certainty, then there is no conception of life having a goal, a directedness of itself: it is then up to me to make my life "meaningful" by setting up my own purpose and working toward it. This is the great gulf between the Semitic religions and those of Indian and Chinese origin. The phrase, "the meaning of life," can be used in connection with these two very different conceptions only by analogy. To those raised under the influence of a Semitic religion, this certainty about important things to come tends to be accepted as a constituent part of religion, to the extent that persons within the tradition of Semitic religions have difficulty in calling a tradition—like Confucianism—which lacks this element, a "religion."

A distinction must be drawn between public or objective realization of the ideal, and the private participation of the individual in it. Public realization of the ideal may be guaranteed, and the participation of the individual highly doubtful, as in many forms of the Semitic religions. The participation of the individual in whatever constitutes "salvation" is usually dependent on the fulfillment of certain conditions by him.

It may be remarked in passing that if we look at the roles played by the ideas of God and the savior in the Semitic religions, that is, if we ask, what does God actually do that would make some experienceable difference, it seems that God is the one who brings about the public or objective realization of the ideal, while the savior makes it possible for the individual to participate in that. Similarly, notions like the *kami* of Shintoism, or *mana*, are assertions that there exists a power capable of solving man's problems with nature, though without any guarantee that it will actually do so for the individual.

b) The second type of assertion about the realization of the ideal solution is a statement about the location or availability of the resources needed to realize it. One option here consists in the conviction that man possesses within himself the resources he needs to achieve the goal. Man can and must save himself. This outlook may be termed "pelagian," and characterizes early and Theravada Buddhism, and Islam. The Buddha could tell his disciples that there is no light to help them other than that which they carry within themselves, but this is sufficient. "Be ye lamps unto yourselves."

The contrasting conviction is that man does not possess the needed resources within himself. He cannot save himself. If he is to be saved, he needs help from outside. This outlook may be termed "saviorist," and characterizes much of Mahayana Buddhism and Christianity. Another alternative is that the resources for the attainment of the goal are contained in nature; this is the view of Taoism, and also, in its own way, of Marxism with its "world-historical process."

The three components mentioned so far constitute the *theoria*, the theoretical aspect of an interpretation of life. Such a theory, however, does not rest in itself; it leads by its nature to action. An interpretation of life implies a way of life. This, too, has components which distinguish one way of life from another.

The elements that comprise a way of life are both evaluative and admonitory. The evaluative element consists in the judgments: (a) that certain things will be considered as values, in an order of priority; (b) that certain actions will lead to the realization of those values; (c) that certain things constitute disvalues, or obstacles to the realization of the values decided upon; and (d) that certain actions will lead to the realization of these disvalues.

The admonitory element consists in the injunction or admonition that the actions believed conducive to the achievement of the values recognized be carried out, and those conducive to the realization of the corresponding disvalues be avoided.

A vision of life does not usually exist in people's minds with the clarity of theoretical structure outlined here: like all vision, it will have, at any given moment, a particular focus, and surrounding that a large, vague field that is intuited rather than seen. But the theoretical elements of the vision are implied in the way of life it proposes, since it is a function of them, and the effectiveness of a religion depends on the adoption of its way of life. There is a tendency, therefore, for religions to lay quantitatively greater stress on the way of life they propose than on the theoretical considerations underlying that way of life.

The yogas of Hinduism, the Eightfold Path of Buddhism, the Jewish Torah, the Islamic Shari'ah are concrete and detailed systems of action that lead to the realization of what in each case are considered to constitute values, according to their priority, and commending the avoidance of other actions held conducive to the realization of what are considered to be disvalues. The same is true, though in a less publicly systematic fashion, of the Christian ethic, and of the behavioral recommendations of the Confucian and Taoist traditions.

Although there is a logical relationship between the various elements of a way of life as outlined here, there is not necessarily any logical connection between the contents assigned to them—in our conception of what constitutes logic. (However, what counts as reasonable argument changes from age to age: an argument that one culture finds convincing may leave a differently cultured mentality unimpressed. The major religions were founded a long time ago.)

The key to understanding a way of life lies in the first step—its assignment of value. This is a derivative of the ideal proposed in the *theoria*. For example, the value assigned to individual human life will vary greatly according to whether the operative ideal is a state of harmony between man and nature, or the overcoming of suffering, or the establishment of just and loving relationships be-tween individuals, or the achievement of nonexploitative social structures. Correspondingly, the imperative to preserve individual human life will have greatly varying degrees of urgency.

Two men in winter look at the side of a mountain covered with snow. What do they see? One says: It is cold, hard and unfriendly; a man might perish there. The other says: The snow is glistening in the sun; look at the soft contours of the rise; and the slope would make a great run for a pair of skis.

One man looks at life, and says: He who knows does not speak; he who speaks does not know.

Another says: Life is suffering; we suffer when we are born, and we suffer when we die. But we suffer because of ourselves, our foolish desires. Let us seek release, abandonment, forsaking, the extinction of craving.

Another says: This life is an illusion; the Imperishable alone is the Real. We are in misery because we have forgotten our oneness with Him who does not die. But truly we are one with Him, and with one another, and with all things, and He is our joy.

Another says: Your hands are full of blood. You cry peace, peace, and there is no peace. Every man is an enemy to his neigh-bor. The good man perishes, and no one lays it to heart. Justice must be done! Share your bread with the hungry, and bring the poor into your house!

The difference between these reactions is not a matter of meta-physics or of history or even of ethics. It is a difference of *vision*. That alone, its vision of life, is what gives any religion its power to move the hearts of men, and claim their inner allegiance.

III

An interpretation of life as outlined here contains no statements about matters of metaphysics or history, about matters of "fact." An attempt must still be made then to deal with the question, what is to be said about such "facts," about the assertion that there exists a Supreme Being, for instance, or that Jesus rose from the dead. It seems that, if I wish to be consistent, I must say that, simply as facts, they become irrelevant to religion. It does not really matter whether in point of fact there exists a personal God or not. What matters is the view of human life which is implied in that idea. It does not matter whether Jesus rose from the dead, or whether there is a future life; what matters is the question of man's dependence on himself, and whether virtue is its own reward. It does not matter whether the Hebrew people left Egypt under Moses or not; the important thing is the special concern for personal relationships which that people developed. It does not matter whether multiplicity is an illusion or not, but that we search for ourselves within ourselves, and not in objects and possessions.

But this is too facile. In point of fact, it matters a great deal if Jesus rose from the dead. Our whole conception of human life and destiny must be altered if such an event actually took place. It matters immensely if Moses received the Law from God. If he did, then there is a certain way of life which has a divine sanction, and which we neglect at our peril. It matters tremendously if multiplicity is an illusion. If it is not, then it may well be that my salvation is to come from some other person than myself, and only on condition that my relationship to other people is different from what my convenience would suggest. But if multiplicity really is an illusion, then it would be foolish of me to look for help anywhere but in the depths of my own being.

It is not possible for us to separate our individual fate from the condition of the world in which we live, and the history which has created it. The realm of objective fact is decisive for our personal existence, it cannot but affect us, make a difference to us, and so be the bearer or destroyer of meaning for us. Conversely, a genuine meaning can only result from some actual state of affairs. It is only possible for a real difference to be made to us if there is something that makes the difference. It may give me great comfort to be assured that my salary is to be raised. But if the company is on the verge of bankruptcy, my comfort is likely to be brief. If my conviction about some improvement in my condition is not to be mere delusion, then there must be objective facts to back it up. A religion is not concerned primarily with facts, but with meanings. But a set of "meanings" lacking reference to an adequate set of facts is fantasy and hallucination. How can I ascertain the facts?

In the normal course of events, when something happens of significance for us, we begin our investigation by ascertaining the facts, and then we try to find out what implications they have for us. We start by reflecting on the objective state of affairs, and then attempt to discover how this state of affairs is going to affect us, what difference it will make to us. When we are dealing with a religion, however, we have to reverse the situation. For here we have to do with a tradition conveying primarily not any knowledge of facts, but a vision of life. The statements in which the tradition expresses itself, despite their appearance of describing fact, function as importative statements. If we wish to discover the original fact, whether historical or metaphysical, which lies behind this particular set of meanings, by the nature of the case the only access we have to it lies through the vision, the interpretation of human life. Instead of beginning with a fact and then trying to ascertain its meaning for us, in a religion we must begin with an interpretation of life, and try to work our way back to whatever metaphysics or history would be needed to support it. I emerged from my front door one morning to discover with dismay a large hole in the sidewalk blocking the entrance to my house. Since I wished to have it removed, I had to discover the cause. Was it a mischievous neighbor, or the sewerage service? On examination I saw it had been dug quite neatly, so I ruled out the mischievous neighbor. Further inspection disclosed a metal box with wires in one corner, so I concluded either to the electricity or the telephone company, and so on. I began with a difference I believed was made to me, and tried to discover the original event behind it.

Something not totally unlike this happens in the case of a religion. The religious tradition provides us, as we have seen, not with a set of primordial or fundamental facts, but with a set of vital meanings. If these meanings are to be genuine, they must derive from some objective facts. Therefore, so long as we are concerned with the religious question, our access to the original facts, that is, to the precise facts which produce these meanings and no others, lies not through historical or metaphysical investigation, but through the meaning patterns that we have inherited. The question as to how we can justifiably assent to a set of meaning patterns without previously ascertaining by some means the truth of the facts which produce them is a further matter and needs more extensive treatment than space allows here. For the moment we are concerned with discovering the facts, having presupposed acceptance of the religious tradition. Since the tradition, as we saw, states meanings, it can only be with them that we begin.

At this point we must recall that a particular meaning can be given by more than one fact. It is possible for any one of a number of different states of affairs to make the same difference.

To return to the lady who ordered the yellow dress for the wedding, and on opening the box exclaims, "This dress is blue," let us suppose her husband takes it on himself to point out that she is in error, that actually the dress is a shade of turquoise. She could be expected to reply, "Well, you idiot, so it's turquoise! That's a great help." It still isn't the color she wants.

Supposing he were simply talking to her on the telephone after she had opened the box, and she said, "I ordered a yellow dress but they didn't send me the color I wanted." If the line then went dead, and he was left wondering what color she did get, there would be two possible answers: either she got some other color than yellow and it won't do, or she got a shade of yellow different from the one she wanted, but it will do.

In other words, there is a wide range of objective facts capable of making the undesired difference, namely, a dress she could not wear ("any color except yellow") , and also a range of facts capable of making the desired difference, a dress she could wear ("some other acceptable shade of yellow") .

A man goes to pick up his automobile from a garage where he has left it for what he considered minor repairs. He emerges from the shop with a bill for $150 and a strong sense of indignation. "This is incredible. They have charged me $50 for labor and $100 for parts." If his wife observes to him, "No, you've made a mistake, dear. They charged you only $50 for parts, and the $100 is for labor," he is likely to feel that his point has been missed. In either event he is still being charged much more than he expected.

While it is true that a genuine meaning can only result from an adequate set of objective facts, it is also true that all sorts of different facts may give a particular meaning. When we are concerned primarily with the difference made to us, the objective fact is of concern only insofar as it makes the difference. As a result there will always be a *spectrum* of possible facts, any one of which could bring about the difference we are concerned with.

The Roman Catholic Council of Trent defined that seven sacraments were instituted by Jesus Christ: not only baptism and the eucharist, of which there is record in the New Testament, but also confirmation and the anointing of the sick, for which there is no evidence whatever that they were instituted by Jesus. Historically speaking, it seems extremely unlikely that Jesus personally informed his apostles that confirmation and the last anointing were "sacraments," or that there were precisely seven of these. If he did, the early Christian church forgot about it promptly, and did not remember it again till several centuries later. What is a Catholic to make of an official statement of his Church like this?

Following our line of argument, he would first have to ask: What is the point of the statement, what difference would it make, if these ceremonies were instituted by Jesus? Perhaps the difference would be that they would have a very special significance for man's relationship to God, a significance not to be gainsaid; they would have an element of definitive seriousness.

Let us suppose, however, that a person is convinced that the establishment of Christianity bears the marks of a divine act, and that such a religion as Christianity naturally expresses itself and has historically decided to express itself, in certain rituals for decisive moments and aspects of a person's life. Would this not be sufficient to give to these ceremonies the same unique force, even if in point of historical fact they were not personally instituted by Jesus?

But if we allow that the principle applies here, that the same difference may be made by a spectrum of very diverse facts, we must also allow it to be applied to more radical questions. The factitive statement that Jesus is the Son of God in a metaphysical sense is a derivative of the meaning statement that he is the savior. The primitive Christian church began with the conviction that Jesus was the savior of mankind, and for a considerable time got along quite well on the idea that he was the Son of God in the moral or adoptional sense familiar to the Hebrew world, as the factual basis for his saviorhood. The encounter with Hellenistic concern for the *eidos,* the idea or essence of a thing, led to the metaphysical conception of his sonship and to the celebrated problem of two Gods in the early Christian church. We must maintain, however, that even in its metaphysical formulation the statement, "Jesus is the Son of God," functions in Christianity not as a metaphysical fact statement, but as a meaning statement, and the meaning it expresses, stated summarily, is: through Jesus men have an assurance of salvation, that is, they have not only the possibility, but the right to hope.

Granted that this, or something like it, is the religious meaning of what has the form of a metaphysical fact statement, "Jesus is the Son of God," we need to inquire, is it necessary in order to preserve the meaning that there is a savior, to conclude that Jesus is the Son of God in the now traditional (since the fourth century) metaphysical sense? Or is it possible that his relationship to God might be defined for a Christian in other terms? We have to say that in principle it is possible, that another set of facts could supply the same meaning and make the same difference, even if at present it is not clear what these other facts might be. Whether some other theory about the relationship of Jesus to God would prove compatible with the Christian tradition will depend on whether it is capable of yielding the same meaning.

But if we are to be consistent we must be prepared not to stop there. The Christian community has lived for a long time on the conviction that there exists a God distinct from the world. This conception has been and is frequently questioned. Taken as it stands, "There is a Supreme Being distinct from the world" is a statement of metaphysics, not of religion, a factitive statement, not an importative one. When it is used as a religious affirmation, however, it functions as an importative one. Therefore the question we must ask is what difference it would make to our interpretation of life if there were a God distinct from the world. As the idea of God functions in the Semitic religions, it could be partly formulated: the ideal of an ethical humanity will one day be realized. (The formulation of this difference is a main task of theology, and demands great care and rigor of thought. Therefore this brief sentence should not be taken as exhausting by any means the possible importance of the idea of a God distinct from the world; it is given only as a example.) But let us agree for the moment that something like this is the meaning of the statement; what metaphysical states of affairs would be incompatible with it, and what would be compatible; what metaphysical states, if any, would be required for it to hold? The Christian tradition has considered a number of quite divergent metaphysical conceptions of God to be acceptable: for example, Augustine's conception of God in terms of Platonic "being itself," Pseudo-Dionysius's idea of God as beyond all being, Aquinas's concept of Pure Act, or Tillich's idea of Ground of Being. Any of these is theologically legitimate for a Christian, but none can be binding on him, because it is not clear that any of them is entailed by the meaning which the Christian tradition assigns to God. On the other hand it seems highly questionable whether the concept of God put forward by Whitehead can fulfill the function of seeing that justice is done, required by the Semitic religions. (That is not an argument against Whitehead; it may be an argument against the Semitic religions.) Likewise the question of the relationship of God to the world cannot be settled, for a religious tradition, on metaphysical grounds. The point of departure must be the interpretation of life that it implies. Theological inquiry about the nature of God or his relation to the world is an inquiry into the range of metaphysical possibilities compatible with a particular religious vision of human life.

To what extent then can a religion or a religious assertion provide us with some information about matters of fact?

First, the width of the spectrum of facts considered able to give the desired meaning or to make this particular difference to people, cannot be settled once and for all beforehand by logical analysis of the meaning itself. If a friend tells me, for example, "I have a newfound confidence in myself," then I know that an important difference has been made to him by something or other. But precisely what it was, or even what general class of experience he has had or discovery he has made, I cannot tell simply from this difference itself. On the other hand, there is one thing that is immediately clear. Whatever it was, it did not (unless he is hallucinating) stand in contradiction to this difference. For example, I would be reasonably certain that it was not because he had just been fired from his job that he had this new confidence in himself, or because his wife had left him (unless the character of his spouse was such as to make that a matter for congratulation) or because he had just received an unusually large income tax assessment.

So, too, with a religious tradition, there will necessarily be some possible states of affairs that would be incompatible with the meaning which forms the heart of the tradition.

The boundaries of the spectrum are set by contradiction. Candidates for the position of the original fact are ruled out if they necessarily yield a meaning which would contradict the meaning in question. But it can be immensely difficult to discover whether a particular fact would necessarily yield such a contradictory meaning. If a man says to me, "I am very happy," and then, when I inquire as to the reason, he informs me, "Because my fiancée has broken our engagement," would I be inclined to rejoice with him or to call the psychiatric hospital?

We cannot always be certain a priori what facts are compatible and what are incompatible with a meaning. The history of Christianity provides abundant examples of beliefs which were once thought to be in contradiction to the meaning of the religion, but were accepted by later generations as compatible with it. There was a time, not very long ago, when a majority of Christians rejected the theory of evolution, especially that of the "simian descent of man," as the plaque commemorating the Scopes trial puts it. They rejected it because they thought, among other things, that the effect of the theory would be to destroy the idea of creation, especially that of the human soul. The idea of creation has the religious function of stressing that the resources out of which man attains salvation are ultimately not his own achievement, but are a gift and are given him gratuitously. The point at issue is a decisive one. But the thinking of Christian men has ceased to consider evolution as a religious problem. The same sort of thing can be pointed out in such issues as the creation of the world in seven days, the sun standing still in the book of Joshua, which brought about the downfall of Galileo, the literary genera of the Bible, the doubtful character of the infancy narratives of Jesus, and so on. In these and in many other cases the general body of the Christian church has come to accept as compatible views which it once considered to be in contradiction to its faith.

But this difficulty is not the peculiar property of Christianity. The world view of the Upanishads is an extreme form of idealism. All the different things we experience, including ourselves, are one with the Absolute, and thus one with each other. This unity of all things in Brahman is their reality. Their individual differentiations are an illusion. A succession of these illusions, in reincarnation, must usually be passed through before unity with Brahman is achieved. The general thrust of the interpretation of life implied in this "nondualist" metaphysical system has already been outlined: man's chief problem in life is himself, more exactly, that part of him which suffers, the suffering self, his own individual existence which lays him open to the painfulness and restrictions of plurality. The ideal solution proposed is the discovery of, and so unity with, the true, hidden self which overcomes the painfulness of plurality. This discovery of one's true self is possible, but not guaranteed; and man possesses within himself the resources needed to achieve it. Would it necessarily be a contradiction of this conviction to reject the vast metaphysical scaffolding of Hinduism, the doctrine that individuality is an illusion, or the accompanying notion of reincarnation? A number of eminent Hindu thinkers have, in fact, abandoned the rigid idealism of the Upanishads for a quite different metaphysics. Dualist and nondualist Hinduism stand in metaphysical contradiction to one another; yet both are now acknowledged as orthodox.

Early Buddhism, though it claimed to eschew metaphysics, and is not commonly considered to rest as a religion on historical events in the sense that the Semitic religions do, still stems from the conviction that Gautama became the Buddha, that he attained enlightenment and Nirvana. Nirvana itself is described in what appear to be metaphysical terms. Also, much of the Buddhist world, both Theravada and Mahayana, retains from Brahmanism a notion, though vague, of reincarnation.

The interpretation of human life which characterizes early Buddhism has been described in outline in the previous section. Life is suffering. But we suffer because of our foolish desires. The remedy lies at hand: release, abandonment, the extinction of craving. That this is the meaning of Buddhism, in the sense in which we have been using the word, is explicitly stated in Buddha's *Sermon at Benares*. We scarcely have any other religion founded so explicitly precisely on an interpretation of life rather than on a set of views about metaphysics or history.

Now when we consider how slight our critical historical knowledge of Buddha is—for example, that the earliest texts of his speeches date from centuries after his death—is it necessary, in order to preserve this hope and even the confidence in these means to achieve it, to insist on the historical figure of Buddha as one who achieved the perfection of enlightenment? Would it be a contradiction of Buddhism as a religion if the doctrine of reincarnation or the belief in the historicity of the Buddha were denied?

The Zen sect of Buddhism, taking its point of departure from devotional Mahayana and the search for union with the Buddha, proclaimed that he was to be found not in devotional practices, but within the heart of the seeker, and came around full circle to an emphasis on contemplation, especially the contemplation of nature; the person of the Buddha has receded into the background altogether in Zen. Are we to decide that Zen Buddhism is not Buddhist? (Practitioners of Zen are given to saying that sort of thing, of course, but such statements are precisely good examples of the importative rather than the factitive use of language. They do not release us from a critical judgment.)

A classic doctrine of Islam is that the Koran was revealed verbally by God to Mohammed. Let us imagine, for the sake of argument, that one day it should be proved beyond all reasonable doubt that the Koran was written some years before the birth of Mohammed. Would such a state of affairs stand in contradiction to the ethical, pelagian interpretation of life which characterizes Islam as a religion? Would Islam as a religion collapse in such an event? Would the millions of human beings whose life is formed and fashioned by it suddenly give the religion up because of a discovery like that?

It was also part of early Muslim orthodoxy that the Koran had existed in heaven from all eternity before it was revealed. Yet the Shi'ite sects have not accepted this, and are not on that count denied the full status of Muslims by their fellows. The mysticism of the Sufis was first hailed as a heresy and persecuted; subsequently it was adopted into Ghazzali's classic synthesis of Muslim theology.

The argument here so far has been that it is not possible to determine *a priori* and once and for all where the boundaries of the spectrum fall, because we cannot tell *a priori* precisely and completely what facts will contradict the meaning of a religion.

People's understanding of the world they live in grows; their horizons widen, sometimes against their will; perhaps their comprehension of their religious tradition deepens, and they come to appreciate a little more adequately the historical processes by which it has developed; and they may become more occupied with its point, with what it is driving at, than with the garments it has decked itself out in in the course of time.

The spectrum of possible facts which will be considered compatible with a religion and capable of making that difference to man of which the religion speaks will vary according to all these factors and others. And so it will vary from person to person, and as far as a religious community is concerned, from age to age, as one understanding of the world, and of what can be reasonably believed, is replaced by another. The significant conclusion of these reflections is that, with regard to the factive statements of a religion, "we have not here a lasting city." Attempts to formulate statements of fact on the basis of a religious tradition can never be final, can never be more than provisional. The present community will be replaced by another generation that understands the world differently, and present efforts to discover how it really was or is will be judged successful to the extent that they will have enabled themselves to be surpassed. Attempts to express the relationship of God to the world, or what actually happened on Easter Sunday, just like conceptions of the way the world began, are and always will be subject to revision.

To say this is to say that factive statements in religion are approximations, destined to give way to closer approximations. That is, they are hypotheses. They are also metaphors. This is an important point, and needs further elaboration. An attempt to state the original fact, whether historical or metaphysical, is subject to revision and refinement. That is one sense in which it is an approximation. Revision and refinement in that case means narrowing the spectrum, so that the field of possibilities becomes more closely defined, and our statement comes closer to the original fact. But it will always be possible to come closer still to the original fact, and so the statement we arrive at is only a better, a closer approximation. For this reason they are hypotheses.

There is another way in which our fact statement is an approximation, namely, that in principle it stands for the whole spectrum of possibilities which could yield the same meaning. It has a representative character, and any other possibility within the spectrum could take its place. The statement that Moses received a revelation on Mount Sinai is supported by the Pentateuch, but so is the statement that he received it on Mount Horeb. Both yield the same religious meaning for Judaism and Christianity. If we utter one, we can do so only if it stands for or represents the other also.

A Christian may say that Jesus rose from the dead with a body that belonged to our customary space and time. Karl Rahner has suggested as an alternative that he rose from the dead with a body that does not belong to our space and time. Each of these is a laudable attempt to say something of interest. But both conceptions fulfill the requirements of the Christian tradition, and either one, in point of fact, when it is made, stands for and represents the entire spectrum of original possibilities. That is to say, it is a metaphor. It is subject to revision in that the other one, and any other one within the spectrum, may some day be considered more likely to yield the meaning and therefore be closer to the original fact.

IV

If we carry through consistently the approach to the theological question outlined here, then the primary concern of the theologian must be to discover and bring to light the *importance* of the doctrine he is attempting to understand and interpret. If it were true, what difference would it make to our interpretation of life? For it is our interpretation of life which is at stake in a religious belief. The *import* of the doctrine or belief is the distinctive vision of life which it implies. I have attempted to give a fairly strict conceptual framework to this notion of a vision or interpretation of life, so that it does not lose itself in fuzziness. Determining a person's vision of life means discovering: (a) what counts for him as man's principal problem in life; (b) what constitutes in his view the ideal solution of that problem; and (c) what the chances and the resources for the realization of that ideal solution are, as he sees it. Admittedly this schema is salvationist in character, that is, it presents any given interpretation of life in terms of the solution to a problem. The question may be raised very legitimately whether there are not some interpretations of life that are non-problematic in this sense. Does it mean, for example, that there are no interpretations of life in heaven? I am reluctant to exclude any reasonable possibility. Yet so long as we are here on earth, it seems to me that our interpretations of life are indeed problematic and salvationist. We have no experience of a life without problems. However, in principle any conceptual framework would be acceptable which gives a recognizable structure to interpretations of life, so that they can be compared and contrasted with one another in some systematic fashion, and the distinctiveness of one brought out clearly in relation to others.

It will be evident that before the import of a belief can be decided, a particular expression of the belief must be taken as the point of departure. In the course of the history of a religion any given belief undergoes changes, more or less drastic, in tandem with the changes that take place in the culture. The same form of words used in two different cultures will very likely have two different significations. Christianity, for example, has maintained a doctrine that Jesus of Nazareth is the savior of the world. But the principal exponents of this doctrine have understood very different things by it. For Justin Martyr, Jesus saves men by teaching them, and what he teaches them is a way of life, in charity and chastity especially. For Athanasius, Jesus saves men by "overcoming death." By his resurrection, Jesus has vanquished death (since people were still dying, however, presumably he meant something like death no longer has final power over us; Jesus' resurrection entitles us to hope for happiness after death). For Anselm of Canterbury, it is neither by his teaching nor by his resurrection that Jesus saves us, but by his death, which restored God's honor, injured by man's sin. For Pascal, Jesus saves us by being the answer to the absurdity of life, though Pascal does not explain how precisely he achieves that. For Teilhard de Chardin, and also for Karl Rahner, Jesus saves us by being the decisive breakthrough in the process of evolution by which God communicates himself to man. For Rudolf Bultmann, Jesus is savior in the sense that the preaching of the message about Jesus calls us to authenticity. For Paul Tillich, Jesus saves us in the sense that the image of Jesus which the New Testament offers us is a model of the "new being" to which we must aspire. It hardly needs to be pointed out that these conceptions of what it is that Jesus does that saves us are different; they are about as different as explanations of any one thing could possibly be.

What then shall we take as our point of departure? It would seem to constitute an ideal solution to this problem if we could discover some structural unity amid this diversity, which would reveal the true significance of the story of Jesus, enabling it to maintain itself over such a long period with such variations. I have in mind the sort of structural analysis which Levi-Strauss suggests for the understanding of a myth. It does not seem possible to apply Levi-Strauss's method exactly as he develops it to the history of theology: we are not in this case dealing with an extended story, composed of constituent units and gross constituent units, as in his dissection of the Oedipus myth. But I wonder whether it would not be possible to develop a related method to uncover the structure of religious convictions which vary greatly over a period of time yet still insist on their continuity, if not identity.

However we do not yet possess in theology any such structural method for dealing with religious convictions and theological positions diachronically and synchronically as he proposes in anthropology. Therefore we must begin somewhere else. I pointed out at the beginning of this essay that the usual place for a theologian to begin his work is with some public objectification of the tradition he is concerned with, which is accepted by the members of the religion as having some special authority, as incorporating the tradition in a specially significant way. In the case of the religion of a literate people, this will usually be found in sacred scriptures.

Thus the natural place for a Christian theologian to take as his point of departure, in the absence of any method for dealing with the tradition as a whole, is the New Testament. In the case of Roman Catholicism it might well be a conciliar, or even a papal definition instead. Or, the subject under discussion may be the appropriateness or acceptability of a particular philosophical or historical position; the question can be raised, for example, of the desirability of adopting a processive conception of God, such as Whitehead's.

In any of these cases, whether we begin with the New Testament, a conciliar definition, or with the convictions of a particular individual, we are dealing with a particular assertion or set of assertions made by a different person from myself, at a different time, in a particular cultural situation. Before we can discover the import, in the sense of the importance, of the assertion, we must discover its literal signification. By this I mean we must find out, as far as possible, what he thought he was saying when he said it. What did he have in mind when he used these words in this way? This would seem to be a simple enough matter in principle, however difficult of execution in practice, a straightforward matter of historical investigation. No doubt that is what is called for. Yet we need to be aware that there is already an act of interpretation involved in this. We are not so much trying to discover what the words mean, because words do not mean anything apart from the person who uses them. Our inquiry is into the mind of the man or men who made or are making the statement we are investigating. The preliminary inquiry concerning the literal signification of the assertion is already a hermeneutical enterprise. I have to re-create the mind of the man who made the assertion. Samuel Laeuchli puts it very well when he says that we must break the past in order to re-create it. I can only understand it from the very different vantage point I now occupy, and so his mind as re-created by me might not be very recognizable to him. My statements about him will implicitly be statements about myself. But then my reason for being preoccupied with him in the first place is to shed some light on my own condition. Of course, that is not the only way of doing history. It is possible to do history out of sheer curiosity. But understood in the existential and self-critical sense which Samuel Laeuchli commends, the historical inquiry is already a theological inquiry. My understanding of my own situation, my vision of life, is not only assumed as point of departure, it is also confronted. In the process I should at least become more aware of it. A thorough historical answer to the question would be at the same time a thorough understanding of myself, of where I stand.

However, it has been the point of this essay that there is a more important question than the historical one. The historical inquiry concerns the past directly, and only indirectly the present. But the question of how I am to interpret life needs to be tackled directly, rather than indirectly. If my interpretation of life is merely assumed as point of departure and used to confront the past, there is a grave and ever-present danger that I will simply read back into the past the presuppositions I start out with. Recently I met two gentlemen who had left their native country and made a trip around the world. I asked their reactions. They replied: We began with the conviction that what we had at home was better than anywhere else, and everything we have seen has confirmed us in that conviction.

In a genuine theological inquiry, my interpretation of life needs to be called into question. This means at the very least that I must ask what interpretation of life is implied in the assertion or conviction under examination. Religious language is not understood until the vision of life which inspires it is understood.

Understood in this light, the idea of a personal God as it occurs in the Judaeo-Christian-Islamic tradition will be viewed primarily not as an abstract metaphysical doctrine now perhaps necessarily superfluous; occurring as it does within ethical religions, it will be seen, among other things, to be the assertion that the ethical salvation that constitutes the ideal solution for man's principal problem, his relationships with other men, will one day assuredly come. That is to say, that justice will finally be done in some sense, and that the actions of men are subject to a final judgment beyond their own. The assertion of God is not a metaphysical speculation, much less the remnant of a myth; it is an assertion of justice, of the necessity of justice, and more than that, of the assurance of justice. In Christianity, this general interpretation of life expressed in the idea of God which it shares with Judaism and Islam is made more specific by the conviction that mankind has a savior, identified with Jesus of Nazareth. Understood along the lines suggested here, christological doctrine, such as that of the two natures, of Jesus, or of his resurrection from the dead, will be seen to be the first instance not as assertions of metaphysics or of historiography, but a set of statements expressing the conviction that, in contrast, for example, to the Islamic view of life, man does not have within himself the resources needed to attain to such an ideal ethical state, or to make himself worthy of it; Christology is the assertion that man cannot save himself. Christology also affects one's precise conception of man's principal problem in life and of the ideal solution to it; for the Christian these must be defined in terms of the preaching of Jesus as we know it. Man's principal problem in life is that he does not live ethically, but what constitutes "living ethically" for the Christian is given by the way of life which Jesus enjoins. It may be remarked in passing that with this approach the problem that has plagued Christian theologians for about a century now, that of the difference between the Jesus of history and the Christ of faith, is in one sense effectively overcome; the Jesus who has been influential in history, the Jesus who affects our interpretation of life as Christians, is the Jesus portrayed in the New Testament. A Christian interpretation of life cannot be timeless and ahistorical; it is linked indissolubly to history; but the historical event to which it is linked is the Jesus who created the Christian tradition, Jesus as he is recorded in the New Testament; if you wish, the historical event to which Christianity is bound is the event of the New Testament—but because of the Jesus whom it contains.

Understood in these terms, the doctrine of a future life has a religious function closely linked to that of the idea of a personal God. Again, it does not function as an assertion of physics or metaphysics. It is an assertion of justice, that justice must be done, that justice will be done, that the actions of man lie under a judgment beyond his own. It is an assertion that man's principal problem in life is not his lack of harmony with nature, nor his experience of suffering, but his relationships with his fellowman; and, most directly, it is an assertion that the ideal remedy for man's situation is a state of affairs where men treat one another properly. While the doctrine of God is an assertion of the certainty that that state of affairs will one day be attained, the doctrine of "the last things," of a future life, is an assertion about the quality or type of that ideal state of affairs: that it is ethical. Again, the notion of "the ethical," of what constitutes "treating one another properly," varies between Judaism, Christianity, and Islam because of their respective convictions that that ideal state is attained through the Torah, through the person of Jesus, or through observance of the Shari'ah. The means qualifies the end.

Once the import, in the sense of the importance, of these factitive beliefs has been brought to light, two significant quesions still remain to be answered, though they are secondary to that main task, from a theological point of view. One concerns the truth of the belief being investigated. By the nature of the case this question cannot refer to the initial, factitive, formulation of the assertion (e.g., "there exists a Supreme Being," or "Jesus rose from the dead"); the truth of a religious belief is a question of the truth of its import, of the vision of life which it implies. The assessment or justification of a vision of life is a matter of peculiar difficulty. In the course of daily life we are constantly making such assessments, but we do not yet possess any agreed methodology for carrying them out reflectively.

The second question concerns the usefulness of the initial factitive and therefore symbolic assertion, and the possibility of replacing it by a more suitable one. Is it still useful to use the term "savior" of Jesus, for example, and if not, what conception could be found that would convey the same religious import to a Christian? Is it still possible to speak of a personal God, and if not, what conception can a member of one of the Semitic religions arrive at that would fulfill the same religious function, have the same import? Answers to this sort of question tend to be determined by the metaphysical presuppositions of the inquirer; and, therefore, these presuppositions need to be carefully examined. It would seem desirable to keep a mind as open as possible to the unimagined possibilities of the universe.

SAMUEL LAEUCHLI

THE DRAMA OF REPLAY

"Do not give to the world one who
wants to be God's; nor cheat him
with matter. Let me receive the
pure light. Once I get there I
shall become man."

Ignatius, Rom. 6.2*

"Then, what is the question?" These final, enigmatic words of
Gertrude Stein phrase the character of the contemporary historical
enterprise, the newest stage in a long process of emerging historical
consciousness. The origins of that process go back to the epoch
when man created his mythological images, Marduk, Noah's ark,
Europa, Indra, and thereby took a first, tentative and stumbling
step toward what later on was to become the historical quest. In a
further development, man took hold of his past more consciously
when he recalled the exodus from Egypt and the wars of Troy
in a poetic mixture of saga and historicity. In an important third
step, he developed his discriminate historical sense: Jeremiah told
the story of Nebuchadnezzar's siege, Thucydides described the war
with Xerxes. In all these stages, however, man did not necessarily
ask why he was turning to the past; he simply began to remember;
he felt the curse of the past and the joy of knowing something
about it; he found out he could use the past to create his future
and to struggle with his peers; above all he began to sense the
value of objectifying his present, both intellectually and artis-
tically, by setting it into perspective with his past. Actually, the
intellectual task of objectifying history and the artistic interpretation of man's personal and social experiences belong together and
have an ancient history: Jeremiah's tortured confessions about
himself and his vivid tales about the fall of the city; Sophocles'
vision of the human tragedy, and Xenophon's story about the
Athenian expedition in Asia Minor. What is new, however, is the

* Seven letters of Ignatius of Antioch are extant and will be referred to in this
essay. They are the letters to the Ephesians (Eph.), Magnesians (Magn.), Trallians
(Tr.), Romans (Rom.), Philadelphians (Phil.), Smyrnaeans (Sm.), and to Polycarp
(Pol.). Wherever these titles or abbreviations are used without further explanation
in this essay, the reference is to Ignatius's letters.

degree of intensified consciousness that underlies the radical sim-
plicity of Gertrude Stein's last question: "What is the question?"
It is the task itself that the contemporary historian must question.
He begins to take cognizance of the fact that in order to achieve
a genuine analysis of the past he must examine the basis from
which he deals with it. So enters what I call the "hermeneutic
consciousness," which is not speculative philosophical fancy, preliminary or postscript to "really serious" historical work, namely,
dealing with "factual" problems, nor is it, as one can hear it dis-
paraged by foes of the once so alive Drew Divinity School, a hobby
of a group of American Heideggerians. To question the historian's
questions is the most urgent critical task of historical scholarship.
By such a hermeneutic task I mean: to examine the place from
which we approach the historical enterprise; to ask for the functional and contextual meaning of the specific historical datum in
a process of analogy that presupposes a proportionality between
the social and personal forces of our contemporary culture and
those of the past; to become conscious of the historical process
that is at work whenever we try to comprehend the past; and to
experience the extraordinary precariousness—shall I say violence
—in one individual's or one group's attempt to encounter and
understand another.

The hermeneutic dilemma, the fact that the questions affect or,
at times, determine the results, is not new, of course. New is the
awareness of the problem and our naming it. The dilemma is
rooted in the tension between the static and mutating aspects of
language in man's cultural evolution. That evolution created a
mind capable of using language as means of expression and interaction. Hence the mind is capable of conceptual constructions that
can be communicated in interactions with other people through
the medium of language. If it were only that simple! But the
evolution of language and the evolution of history proceed un-
evenly. Even in the formation of the personality, the child, for
the most part, learns an immense vocabulary for which it is not
ready; in turn, many an adult goes through experiences for which
he does not yet have language, and in that case his experiences
outrun the capacity of his language to express them. The tension
between experience, social reality, and language is built into the

very fabric of our history, both personal and general. Fairy tale means something different to the three year old, the ten year old, and the forty year old. The forty year old cannot become a three year old again. But he can, through an extremely sophisticated and imaginative process—the kind of intuition exemplified in the work of Piaget, for instance—attempt to recapture what "fairy tale" might mean to the three year old. It is the same with man's attempt to recapture the past. Language and experience are in constant, unequal flux, and that flux produces the hermeneutic dilemma. That being so, it is inevitable and necessary that the questions through which man approaches his past change. His methodology changes in response to his experiences of life. Philo could not take the myths of Genesis literally, so he designed a method of coping with them, and the method, as we know, consisted of a process of explaining the myths by hypostatic, metaphysical images: he changed his way of dealing with the past. Ever since Philo, ever since Deuteronomy and Thucydides, historical methodology, that mixture of detachment and involvement, has undergone one change after another, expressing and contributing to the historical evolution. Medieval man dealt differently with patristic material than did the Renaissance scholar—witness, for instance, the impact made by the fifteenth century discovery of the fictional character of the Donation of Constantine. Again, historians of the eighteenth and nineteenth century approached the same patristic material from quite a different perspective— witness the importance of skepticism toward miracle and myth. Only naive fundamentalist or positivistic scholars can ignore the fact that questions—methodologies!—change because they are rooted in the ongoingness of history. What is new, I repeat, is that we are increasingly conscious of the methodological problem, which means we try to say *which* questions are crucial at our specific moment in time.

There are basically four factors that I regard as essential to an understanding and description of the present stage of historical consciousness. Of first importance, a new attitude is emerging as to what "historical understanding" can mean; not lesson, kerygma, or illustration, but an awareness of historical confrontation as more than a mere act of description. Man does not merely describe; he re-creates. And in that re-creation he is aware of his involvement; he wants to comprehend, but he knows that comprehension demands that he impose structures and patterns on the historical material. He is aware of the tension between comprehension and confrontment; he feels the distance and limitations. Aware of the clash of epochs and of cultural frameworks, he experiences his inability to bridge them. Even if he cannot definitely solve the historical problem, *precisely* because he cannot solve it, he acknowledges it and faces it. The positivist wanted to describe the object; the existentialist wanted to eliminate the distance between himself and the object. I, however, begin my work consciously acknowledging that the gap cannot be fully bridged and in realizing this fact I experience my own historicity. The second factor to consider is the ethical relativism in historical evaluation. In both mythical and critical thinking, the past tended to be either ideal or nightmare: *aurea prima aetas*, the Mosaic age of revelation, the unique age of the apostles, the charismatic decades of the Reformation; or the age of medieval darkness, the repressive governments of Nero and Domitian, the centuries of human exploitation. Such dichotomies of black and white do not correspond to the nature of our experiences, and the recognition of such mixture and fluidity alters historical thinking significantly. Values have always shifted: for Luther, Thomas Aquinas was "bad" and Huss was "good"; for the Marxist, Luther was "bad" and Thomas Müntzer was "good." But such distinctions themselves have become blurred—we think of the contemporary novel or drama—or at least, new qualitative differences other than traditional ethical or social ones are drawn on. We do not ask: Who is good and bad, or who is right or wrong? Instead we ask: Where lies creativity, even though this creativity may come forth from ambivalent humanity and be destructive as well as forming? The third factor I must reckon with is the problem of man's cultural mutation. Although man remains basically the same physiologically, he changes emotionally, culturally, and intellectually. The study of the past deals with the same anatomical human species, but it has to reckon with a continual mutation in man's technical proficiency, in his interpersonal relationships, in his intellectual development, in his awareness and consciousness.

Fourth, I must deal with the ambiguity of words. Language is not what it has been assumed to be for so many thousand years, a direct, unequivocal, and static transmission of events and ideas. A word not only reveals, it hides. What makes the historical enterprise so difficult is this combination of the problematic of mutation with the problematic of language: the persons and events of the past are no longer accessible to check or control. Yet it is precisely the remoteness of the historical material—my experiencing history as mutation—that helps to create the "historical perspective."

At the beginning of the second century, Ignatius of Antioch wrote seven letters as he traveled through ancient Asia Minor. The letters illustrate the methodological problem. The cities to which he wrote and through which he passed still exist, either in ruins—Ephesus, Sardes—or as modern cities—Smyrna, Rome. The fact of their cultural mutation is obvious. The cities that live today are not what they were in Ignatius's time. The agora of Smyrna has been excavated and some marble columns and inscriptions remain as monuments, some from the very age of Trajan when Ignatius passed through the city. But quite another city lives now around that agora, a bustling seaport of some 400,000 people. The old Smyrna has become Izmir. The Ionians and Romans have been replaced by the Turks. In order to re-create the city as it was under Trajan, I must, somewhat like the archeologist, dig under the surface; I must discard as well as reconstruct.

But the problem of mutation is much more serious still. I am talking about the letters of Ignatius of Antioch, the *man* Ignatius of Antioch. There is no direct analogy between me and Ignatius, and hence there is no direct access from me to him. The man is dead. I cannot interview him, play back a videotape, talk to his friends or his foes. All I have to go on are his words. But his words are extremely problematic, as problematic as my own words. Sometimes, perhaps, words have done an adequate job. Frequently, however, words confuse the issues. They are ambivalent; and they are ambivalent because in the act of creating words, or expressing feelings in words that are meant to communicate, the speaker veils as well as reveals. Furthermore, words not only express, they lie and deceive. I cannot assume that when Ignatius wrote he always did an adequate job with his words, with "death" (*thanatos*), "unity" (*henosis*), "Lord" (*kyrios*), or "savior" (*soter*); or that when he wrote he expressed his belief and gave statements of fact. Instead I must acknowledge that his words were expressions of social interplay, that they may include evasions, expectations, illusions, that in his words he may have manipulated, tried to talk himself into what he did not deeply experience; that his words were at times precisely what he felt or meant, but that they were also at times imperfect expressions of what he felt or what he intended to say. It is bewildering, indeed, to consider the extraordinary complexity, dialectic, inadequacy, if not to say deception, in the words I encounter.

On the other hand, I am dealing with a concrete product of a concrete event. That event was a physical reality. A Christian from Antioch on the Orontes River in Syria, held captive by a group of Roman soldiers and sent to Rome for some crime of lese majesty, wrote or dictated a series of letters. That writing, or dictation, was an *action*. Christians had come from Ephesus and other cities to pay a visit to the traveler; to these Christians Ignatius talked. He tried to communicate, he wrote. The action took place in the midst of countless other actions, of slaves loading and unloading ships at the seaport; of workers building and rebuilding streets and houses and temples under the new aggressive administration of the great successor of Nerva. However, what has come down to us is not the action itself, not the motion of human bodies, the sound of words, or even the imprint of the hand that put down the words. What has come down is a single consequence of that action, the verbalization and reflection of it in the words. The action itself is lost; perhaps Ignatius wept, fell down, laughed, raised his hands, perhaps he spoke quietly while his body shook. Only written words are extant to testify to that action. In these words the man expressed himself and interacted with his visitors and his addressees. The words are all I have with which to reconstruct the action, a fusion of self-expression and social interplay which went on as Ignatius wrote or dictated. I am therefore confronted by the task of returning to an action that can only be grasped in its verbal aspect and only through the words of one side.

It is to that duality between Ignatius's words—which have survived and can be analyzed—and Ignatius's actions—which can merely be inferred from their verbal expressions—that I try to return in historical work. The task is an extremely complicated process of repetition, reaction, comprehension, reenactment, and interpretation. Just as Ignatius's words were not merely a static abstract statement of belief or truth, so my own sequence of historical reenactment is not merely abstract. It is itself an event: I read the text, which is a physical as well as an intellectual event; I examine the Greek words; I drive over the roads from Ephesus to Izmir and Pergamum and follow Ignatius on his journey; I use every means at my disposal to capture the social dynamic of his age; I try to enter the dream world of terror and hope that comes out in the words of the tortured man. My own words are part of my actions and hence my historical approach to Ignatius cannot be severed from my own social context, my emotions, my history.

In order to outline that complicated and multilinear process of historical understanding and confrontation, I propose five steps through which such reenactment can be essayed. I am not writing a full monograph on Ignatius since a detailed analysis would transcend the purpose of this book. I want to propose paradigms with which to operate in historical research, paradigms which are applied in and are part of a sequence of reactions. Why talk about Ignatius of Antioch, then, and not merely about stages and paradigms? Because a methodology described in the abstract is unsatisfactory, not only because in history, as well as in life and art, form can never be fully separated from content and vice versa, but because the methodological guidelines I am about to present reckon concretely with the fact that the observer reacts spontaneously to concrete historical material; that such reaction is open-ended; and that the reaction represents—at least potentially—an event. I do not mean to say that the paradigms I am about to present are only applicable to Ignatius of Antioch. I would certainly approach Augustine, Thomas Aquinas, or Karl Barth with similar methods. But the reaction to Karl Barth would not be the same as to Ignatius. The five steps cannot always be neatly followed, of course; they are meant to serve as experimental framework through which to understand what goes on in the historical enterprise. It is that task, in the midst of the crisis of historical scholarship, I want to affirm: that it is not only interesting and worthwhile, but crucial to face history, to distance oneself from the past—instead of embracing or dismissing it—in order to experience it; to re-create the past in order to understand it. I affirm that task by becoming conscious of what I am doing and by experimenting with new structures of research.

I

In the first stage of my methodology I try to become conscious of the cultural, intellectual, and personal framework from which I start my work. More is not possible. What we do is frequently ahead of what we *know* we do. Like any novel, painting, or sculpture, the historian's work is, to a certain degree, beyond his own consciousness and can be fully understood only in retrospect. But the attempt to fix the point of departure must be made because in historiography we are dealing not merely with an artistic process but with a critical-intellectual one as well. To know where we are implies that we can say where we have been; that we are no longer there; that we experience exactly *not* identity, but transformation and metamorphosis. The cosmos of Ignatius of Antioch is not the cosmos of a space age, of multimedia electronic transmission, of microbiological experiments creating life.

The starting point is a new one; in my case a pluralistic twentieth century multiuniversity, a department of religion in the midst of a chaotic, tumultuous, urban ghetto within a crisis-laden, fragmented, democratic culture. The starting point can be defined as post-Nietzschean, post-Marxist, post-Freudian—I am inclined to add: post-Heideggerian and post-Wittgensteinian. I use the prefix "post-" because the starting point, the present, is defined by the past, by forces which formed us and from which we are in the process of liberating ourselves. I start in a cosmos of cultural pluralism, brought about by a rapid and unorganic mingling of traditions, races, and religions; of spatial consciousness, which gave the death blow to vertical images of life; of absurdity, phrased by poets and painted by artists, the result of new sensitivities toward war and injustice; and of entirely new means of communication.

The great period of German scholarship, for instance, from F. C. Baur to Harnack and Lietzmann, took for granted a common basis of scholarship, a basis from which some "bigots" were excluded, to be sure, and from which certain "dreamers" were laughed at, but a consensus from which the academic "conversation" was carried on. That basis was the aristocratic humanistic climate in a German university, a powerful force in eighteenth and nineteenth century Europe from Kant to Hegel. What has to be faced is the end of this cultural framework, the breakdown of the traditional universes of discourse. The university from which I start my examination is no longer a unity, a "campus." Instead I find myself in a wilderness of possibilities—a web of sociological, behavioristic, anthropological, historical methodologies which are not only ways of coping with life, but means of distinguishing one group, and one individual, from others. Logical positivists blast the existentialists' philosophy as confused, historians scoff at the perversity and subjectivity of the psychologists, and the behaviorists laugh at the "hang-ups" of the Freudians: they are engaged in a struggle for power in a divided university, but they also reflect the conflicts of the society at large as much as those within and between academic groups. Knowledge belongs to cultures, to special groups, to teams of individuals. It is romantic to believe that the scholars of Heidelberg and of the Sorbonne in the year 1880 were free of such socio-intellectual interdependence. Harnack did not know the mind of Overbeck; he fought for his position as Germany's patristic genius and he was threatened by Overbeck both emotionally and socially. The problem of pluralism and academic relativism, in which fragmentation and alienation are inescapably embedded, was always part of academic history. However, in the second half of the twentieth century, the extent of the fragmentation has become extraordinary. We *have* to take seriously the sociology of knowledge; and we cannot even act *as if* a common basis existed.

I start with the full knowledge of the hermeneutic problem, aware of the relationship between historical knowledge, interaction, and experience. Take, for example, a seminar on Ignatius of Antioch. It is an illusion to think that a group of graduate students and scholars can sit around a table examining the letters of the bishop of Antioch detachedly, abstractly. When we enter the room, we bring along the conflicts and involvements of our own past, including even what has transpired in the immediately preceding hour or two. These conflicts and involvements are not merely peripheral, as one might think; they are actively at work, although frequently concealed and unacknowledged, as shaping influences in the process of understanding. In the past years I have had many rabbinical students in my seminars. The Israeli-Arab war and the problem of Jewish identity in the United States were present. By "present" I mean they were major factors in each student's participation. The seminar cannot be severed from the cultural turmoil, just as my own writing of this essay cannot be separated from my own life. Because my mind is part of my body, and my personality exists in an ongoing context, research reflects and responds to contemporary issues. The event at Smyrna becomes an event at Philadelphia, Pennsylvania. There is always— and not merely peripherally—a crucial element of involvement present in dealing with history; the encounter with the past is at the same time an intense, often indirect, struggle with the present.

An example would be helpful here. F. A. Schilling wrote a book on Ignatius of Antioch in which he attempted to safeguard the martyr from psychological categorization (*The Mysticism of Ignatius of Antioch*). The attempt, to be sure, is not too well done and strikes one as simplistic and apologetic; it simply affirms that the death wish does not exist and that the man from Antioch was not self-destructive and masochistic. Yet Schilling's 1932 dissertation demonstrates my case. His refusal to accept psychological categories in dealing with Ignatius was a direct response to the rejection of psychological categories in his own life. Before him Lightfoot and Streeter had applied such categories to Ignatius and had seen masochistic elements in the martyr's letters. Donald Riddle's psychological insights and Schilling's rejection of such insights in the historical document are both genuine responses, however. They reveal or unveil the historical present. What separates these scholars are by no means some subjective peripheral notions, but their conflicting views on human behavior. The historian has every right, of course, to protest the use of such terms as "masochism," "canopy," "stimulus," or "death wish." Scholarship partakes in evolution, but the individual does not have to accept every theory of that evolution. However, the historian should not fool himself into believing that to skirt the dangerous social or psychological categories gives him greater objectivity.

These are some of the factors to consider as I fix the point of departure for my intellectual, social, personal, and political context as a period of rapid change, of a crisis in our culture which is responsible for the crisis in historical scholarship. Positivistic and existentialist structures no longer function, while a seemingly radical iconoclastic movement naively pretends to eliminate history, to be able to live without history. Crisis situations, T. S. Kuhn pointed out (in *The Structure of Scientific Revolutions*), bring about scientific revolutions which consist in trying out new paradigms when old ones no longer function satisfactorily. Patristic as well as other religious studies have all too long neglected to respond to the crisis positively and to deal with the past in new ways. How does one determine the sufficiency of proposed new structures? How does one know if they will contribute to a better understanding of Ignatius, as well as to our own intellectual and cultural development? It would be foolish to answer that question summarily when the specific revolution has hardly begun. *Traduttore traditore*, the Italians say, and that maxim is valid not only for the process of translation from one language to another, but for the possibility of communication from one age, and one individual, to another. To understand anyone, anything, is precarious, tentative. And yet I want to try, with R. D. Laing (*The Politics of Experience*) who comprehends so profoundly the lack of continuity between different human experiences:

> Yes there are moments
> Sometimes
>   there is magic.

II

My second step, turning from an analysis of the point of departure to the object, is to lay out the background from which Ignatius of Antioch came. No man is born into a vacuum but into a history, a context. The possible extent of that history is immense, of course: man's entire civilization all the way back to the caves and even to the jungle. There is an immediate history, however, and it is to that immediate period I must limit myself. But even here, the possibilities are legion; one could write a ten-volume work every time one introduces a historical figure—volumes on religious, social, economic, philosophical questions, in Ignatius's case on the New Testament, the city of Antioch, the province of Syria, Jewish diaspora. I must limit myself. The historical introduction is an act of choice determined by the vision of the interpreter, a reduction performed by the man who enters the historical drama. Even here, in the presentation of the background, a false objectivity must be replaced by the conscious admission that reduction of the material is an act of interpretation and belongs to an authentic historical confrontment. In the following paragraphs, I point to the fields of historical contexts with which I must deal as I approach Ignatius.

There is a geographic context: Ignatius came from western Syria. He addressed communities in Asia Minor and Rome. The entire action occurred within a narrow geographic span, namely, the trade route from Antioch to Rome, first inland over Asia Minor to Ephesus and then north by way of the sea. All of Ignatius's letters were written to churches along that exceedingly narrow path, none to churches outside of it, except the letter to Rome, the capital toward which he headed. He did not write a letter back to the church of Antioch, or if he did that letter is lost.

An urban context: Antioch, with its several hundred thousand inhabitants, the third largest metropolis of the empire, a vital Hellenistic center in the province of Syria, bridge between Mesopotamia and the West. The cities of Asia Minor, heirs to an age-old Greek civilization, now under Roman domination. Rome, holding "the first place in the country of the land of the Romans" (Rom., salutation), the city with a strong Christian community that attracted Ignatius, judging from his exuberant address, more than all the others. In these cities, various social strata struggling with each other for survival under imperial rule: traditional municipal aristocratic families, being pushed aside by a new elite, the imperial administrative and military power structure; the active mercantile class, carrier of the important East–West trade, a cosmopolitan stratum in which Christians from Rome traveled east, believers from Smyrna moved to Lyons, theologians from Pontus, Syria, and Egypt visited churches in Ephesus and Rome; minority groups from the countryside as well as from other provinces, Jewish as well as Graeco-Roman; professional people, slaves. In these cities, an urban pluralism, reflected by religious and ethnic varieties, thrived. To such urban communities Ignatius wrote, in Greek to be sure; he took it for granted that the Christians in the city would be able to read his letters as they had read Paul's.

A political context: the principate under Trajan. The oppressive age of Domitian replaced by a new humane atmosphere under Nerva and the rather spectacular rule of his adopted son, under whom Rome enjoyed the greatest territorial expansion of its entire twelve-hundred-year history. Military success in Dacia and Arabia. Pyrrhic victories over Persia. Trajan's splendid personal achievements leading to his title *optimus princeps* in A.D. 114. A year later he came to Antioch, and it would be illuminating to know if Ignatius wrote before or after that visit. The letters supply no clues. Everywhere in the empire, political propaganda about the greatness of Rome and the divine origins of its emperors. In Priene, an inscription praised the good news about Augustus's birthday; in Smyrna, a marble block in the agora contained a dedication to the savior Trajan.

An economic context: remarkable achievements of Trajan's reforms. Peasants allowed to burn their debts. Orphans protected. New buildings everywhere in the empire. A highway from Asia Minor to the Euphrates River. The mercantile class gained from the boom. Immense wealth in Daphne outside Antioch. But the poverty of the lower classes and of the countryside still not eradicated. Trajan not as successful as he thought he was. And the war with Persia was foolish.

A legal context: Pliny, governor of Bithynia, wrote to Trajan asking what he should do with a crazy sect that called itself "Christian." The emperor's reply was ambivalent, Roman, pragmatic: Do not seek them out, do not listen to anonymous denunciations, but should you capture a Christian kill him if he refuses to sacrifice; let him go free immediately if he does sacrifice. The legal context was extremely opaque: What status did the Christian sect enjoy? Was it prohibited? A collegium? On the same legal terms as the synagogue? Was it totally ignored? The Romans were uncertain about the kind and degree of danger from this new religious movement. The uncertainty was reflected in the legal attitude.

A religious context: an aggregation of different religious strata existing in juxtaposition, from primitive magic to sophisticated philosophical theology. Native local cults; tribal remnants, traditional mythic religions supporting municipal power. The crisis of these religious forces as a result of urbanization, syncretism, science, and technology, as a result of philosophical critique, poetic awareness, and a beginning historical consciousness. Ever since Augustus the empire had attempted to revive the old gods but it had also created its own new myth about its *divus imperator*. Temples to Roma, Augustus, and Saturn everywhere. A tendency to stem the religious crisis by a return to primitive rural symbolism, as if perhaps the power found in blood and water might counteract the threatening momentum of urban civilization. Architectural creativity expressed a religious inversion: formerly in the emphasis on external space, the Parthenon, the Jupiter temple on the Capitoline Hill, the Yahweh temple in Jerusalem—symbols of tribe, *polis*, *urbs*, and *orbis*, presenting themselves to the world, with an outside altar and a public ceremony; now in an emphasis on the internal space, Rome's Orphic *basilica sottoterranea*, the synagogue, the Mithraic *spelaeum*, the Christian house church— sanctuaries built to house private sects with their exclusive rituals and their special theologies.

A psychological context: in the urban mass culture the antique form of alienation. Ancient man was lost, erring, caught between conflicting ethnic customs and between different mythic traditions, and he tried to adjust to urban civilization by seeking arcane experiences. He joined groups claiming revelatory insights to give him a social identity as well as a theological canopy; he looked for immortality, rebirth, new life, eternal salvation; he demanded unity, on a philosophical, political, or mythic level, because his world had fallen apart; he was susceptible to ideas that separated body and mind. He lacked strength to sustain the tangible chaos of his age, or at least, he became aware of the chaos in which man

found himself on earth. Yet the crisis caused by such urban, intellectual as well as technological, changes had also begun to bring
some sense of individuality, among some of the great dramatists,
poets, philosophers, and theologians of antiquity, a heightened
awareness: the unexamined life was indeed no longer worth living.

The context was Jewish: in Antioch, as well as in the cities
addressed and visited by Ignatius, extensive diaspora communities,
containing a wide spectrum of cultural characteristics. Pious observers of the Torah. Radicals, praised in Fourth Maccabees, an
ancient "Palestinian Liberation Front." Ascetic groups, the members of which lived a disciplined life, as exemplified by the *Manual
of Discipline*. Half-emancipated Jewish citizens of the Hellenistic
cosmos, ready to live both as faithful members of the synagogue
and as somewhat reluctant participants of the imperial culture.
Fully emancipated Jews who might have ordered a pagan tomb-
stone with a menorah, revealing their deep absorption of the
Graeco-Roman culture. There was not just *one* Jewish context;
there were different Jewish groups creating various contexts. Yet
the war of A.D. 66–70 had left tragic wounds for all involved, and
under Trajan new tensions arose, and new imperial actions, brutal
and determined, were taken.

The context was Christian: for seventy or eighty years, in Antioch as well as in other cities of Asia Minor, flourishing congrega-
tions which called themselves "Christian." They had a new hope:
Christ was risen from the dead and was to return. They saw
themselves as a new race. They shared a new experience, with a
rich new imagery, with rituals taken over from Judaism and pagan
movements. But they also had been, practically from the beginning, in conflict with each other. In the Book of Revelation,
written only shortly before Ignatius was captured, the churches of
Asia Minor are shown in bitter strife, personal (Jezebel!) as well
as communal ("if you were at least cold!"). In the pastoral Epis-
tles, written similarly just prior to Ignatius's own time, the
churches were shown trying to find a viable form of church
government, monarchic in fact. Context meant: Christians against
Christians.

Context: intimate communal groups. Mystery cults; Orphic
sects; Mithraic communities, with their rituals and numinous

symbolism. Pseudo-religious societies. Collegia. Pythagorean in-groups. Philosophic circles. Catechetical schools. Funeral societies.

Context: at Ephesus, the library of Celsus, symbol for the cli-mate of learning, of sharing information, of remembering man's discoveries and myths. Outside the same city, the enormous temple to Artemis with the famous statue of the goddess, crowned, dis-playing the breasts of fertility, her gown covered by animals, queen of Asia Minor's forest. In the synagogue of Sardis, a Cybele stone.

Context: Roman officials, at times corrupt, at times with high standards, as in the case of Pliny. Lawyers, priests, old-fashioned priests of the old gods, newfangled priests of the imperial cult and its councils. Members of the widespread bureaucracy of the im-perial power structure reaching into almost every sphere of daily life. Scholars who interpreted Homer. Astronomers who had insights which were to be celebrated fifteen hundred years later as spectacular new discoveries, as for instance the planets' rotation around the sun and the tipped axis of the earth. Philosophers divided into many schools. Cynic-Stoic preachers on the street corners, proclaiming new ways of life. Prophets. Rabbis with their followers.

Context: amphitheaters, arenas, fora teeming with people. Huge crowds of slaves in overcrowded cities. Baths. Brothels. Temples. Nymphaea. Taverns. Bread shops, wine shops, olive shops. Harps. Athletes. Pulleys. Leopards.

Context: a world of superstition and magic. The evil eye. Astrology. Demons. Witches. Papyri sold for various purposes, to heal, to make love, to destroy. Drugs, potions. Medicines.

Context: in the urban melting pot built of brick and marble and of human crowds struggling for survival and asking for the circus and the bread, the *pax Romana*, a spectacular if deficient achievement of temporary stability.

III

It is not enough to outline a man's context in order to compre-hend from where he comes. Ignatius used words. Few words appear *ex nihilo*. Yet neither do they come from this or that particular context, from this or that community or individual.

Most often, words come from several heritages, from a confusing background of seemingly opposite traditions. Take, for instance, the word *kyrios* met frequently in the letters of Ignatius. That word did not belong to any one tradition nor did it mean one specific thing. In daily life, it could mean a master, a patron; in Jewish contexts, the Lord, Yahweh; in primitive Christian circles, either God or Jesus Christ; in imperial propaganda, the emperor, in political or historical texts, a king or ruler.

It does not help, therefore, to ask: Was the word which Ignatius inherited Jewish, early Christian, political-pagan? Similarly, it does not help at all to ask: Which of Ignatius's words were Gnostic and which were primitive Christian? Take the word "silence," for instance, which appears in Ignatius. Later in the century it became an archetypal concept for some Christian writers whom the Christian polemic and modern scholars call "Gnostic." But the word was used in daily life: there can be silence between people. The word could also have come to Ignatius as the phrase of some mystic group practicing liturgical silence. The word could have existed in the early Christian church as a heritage from the Old Testament, the Psalms. Very few words were ever "Gnostic" as such, least of all in this period where what later on became Gnostic terms were used by Christian and Jewish as well as pagan writers.

It does not help to ask: Which words were Hellenistic and which were in the "Old Testament tradition"? Such an apologetic way of phrasing the problem of heritage is based on erroneous comparisons between eighth century B.C. prophetic texts—which represented only one segment of eighth century B.C. Jewish culture!—and first century documents—which again only reveal some particular groups and individuals within Judaism. Nor does it help to ask: Which words were authentically Christian? There existed Christian models, to be sure: Jesus Christ, the risen one; but the vast bulk of primitive Christian vocabulary was not indigenous. Ignatius came from a Christian community and wrote to Christian communities; but the words he used were as much related to non-Christian as to primitive Christian traditions. When we isolate "authentically Christian" words in Ignatius's background we merely decide, in retrospect, what we would like to see as "authentic" in primitive Christianity.

Instead I propose to approach Ignatius's heritage by asking two kinds of questions about the kind of language he learned to use and about the problems he took on by using such language. In order to understand both the socio-linguistic dynamic behind the man and the individual creativity in him, I must first ask some historical-biographical and secondly some analytic-structural questions about his linguistic heritage.

How did Ignatius receive his words? A number of words seem to be his own creation, composites expressing his Christian identity: "the God bearer" (*Theo-phoros*), "the Christ bearer" (*Christo-phoros*). For the rest he used words he had either heard or consciously learned. These words were Greek; the style is native Greek. He came from Syria, but from Greek-speaking Syria. His educational and social background as clearly revealed in the letters was the middle class of Syria, and certainly not the poor. Ignatius did not write like an ignorant peasant or slave, nor did he betray senatorial or equestrian traits in his upbringing. Nothing in his style betrays a direct relationship to the rebellious classes of Syriac-speaking Syria, the circles that produced a man like Tatian half a century later. Ignatius learned his language from Greek schoolmasters; he had been taught to use grammatical constructions; to write a greeting at the beginning of a letter (Sm., salutation) and a farewell at the end (Phil. 11.2); he had been formed, either by direct schooling or by being exposed to people representing the educational achievement of Graeco-Roman civilization, by typically ancient rhetoric: "Stand firm as an anvil that is smitten!" (Pol. 3.1).

What about his reading? With so little source material available to us, the question is hardly answerable. As with most of us, a great deal of material which he read was ignored or forgotten or just never appeared in his writing. However, it is possible to ask what evidences of literary sources appear in the document. It seems clear that Ignatius had read part of the Gospel of Matthew (Matt. 10.16 in Pol. 2.2 for instance), and some of Paul (1 Cor. 15.8–9 in Rom. 9.2). It is possible, of course, that Ignatius merely heard parts of Matthew and Paul from individuals in Antioch. More significant yet is the question: What does *not* appear in these letters? The Gospel of John, for instance, and the Old Testament. One might easily conjecture that he had read both but simply did not let them surface enough to be identified. However, Ignatius was so extremely anxious to express *unity* that it is unlikely he would have passed up the chance to quote John or Ephesians had he read them or heard about them. Despite some allusions to Jewish practices and to Moses, the prophets and the Law, Ignatius did not know the Old Testament well. The lack is significant. There is anti-Jewish polemic in his letters, and plenty of it. For polemic purposes writers of the ancient church loved to make use of Old Testament images, and understandably so. It was, as exemplified by Paul, 1 Clement, Barnabas, Justin Martyr, an almost indispensable tool in the controversy with the synagogue. Ignatius, therefore, cannot have grown up in a Septuagint-diaspora community, nor can he have lived very long in a Christian congregation that was familiar with Old Testament models.

One can also ask: How did the man learn to use language? To what groups and sources were his linguistic expressions related? Sometimes a clear answer can be given. Ignatius employed a rhythmic hymnic style which he had received from the Christian community (Sm. 1 and Tr. 9). The style, to be sure, is related to a large tradition of Near Eastern hymnody, but the creedal form of expression in his letters undoubtedly came from the specific liturgical *locus* in the Christian tradition. More often, such clear answers cannot be given. Ignatius's style was influenced by the aphorisms of popular philosophy: "Mark the seasons!" (Pol. 3.2). He could have learned such phrases from Cynic-Stoic philosophers in Antioch; he could also have received them from a mystery teacher or from a presbyter in the Christian community: "Be diligent!" (Pol. 3.2). Ignatius also had learned to express himself in the imaginative play of mythological poetic language (Eph. 19), in the rhythmic concentration of models by asyndetic parallelism (Eph. 7). Neither of these patterns belongs to a specific tradition, however; they appear in primitive Christian texts, Pauline letters for instance, but they also are found in Jewish as well as in pagan Near Eastern documents of the imperial age.

Furthermore, one could ask: Which language models that one might expect to find in Ignatius's letters are, in fact, rarely used or even absent? Referring to the scholarly debate on the so-called

Gnostic problem, I must answer: typically Gnostic models, i.e., models reminiscent of Valentinus, the Apocryphon of John, Basilides, or the Gospel of Truth, are certainly not common. Ignatius was not brought up by a community that later on produced the kind of literature found at Chenoboskion. I have already mentioned the fact that he did not come up through a congregation that had deep Jewish roots.

Or one could ask: What unexpected language models appear in his writings? Word constructions reminiscent of mystery cults. Ignatius created several composites: "the Christ bearer" (*Christo-phoros*), "the God bearer" (*Theo-phoros*), "the temple bearer" (*nao-phoros*); he had learned such linguistic combinations from somewhere outside the Christian community. Cults from Asia Minor used such combinations to designate their initiates: "tree bearers" (*dendro-phoroi*), for example.

These few indications point to a Greek-speaking background, non-Jewish, related to popular philosophy, in competition with the synagogue. I suggest that there is a real possibility Ignatius may have been a convert, as shown not only by his limited knowledge of Old Testament material but by his *Christo-phoros* creation; he might have been a member of some other cultic group at one time. In any case, Ignatius represents a background only peripherally touched by the diaspora.

Words make a precarious biography. In cases where a great deal of material or even autobiographical works have survived, as with Luther or Augustine, the biographical approach can be somewhat more successful. Yet even then the approach is limited and other methods must be devised to understand, to sift out a writer's heritage. Instead of only asking what Ignatius read and which persons and communities influenced him, I also ask: What linguistic problematic did he inherit? In any given period of history man inherits the built-in ambiguity of language, its inconsistency, its potential for separation and conflict.

Linguistic ambiguity reveals the structures of society, but it also hides and conceals the individual's experiences. It is that ambiguous character of language that permits the observer to enter into the dynamic of a culture because that ambiguity, built into the structure of speech, reveals the social and individual dialectic of an age, the specific tensions between what man wanted and what he found in his social reality, the conflicts between ideal and daily life, the discrepancy between what men say they are and what they actually do. The ambiguity of words is the key to the past.

Such ambiguity existed from the beginning in the Christian experience itself and appeared everywhere in Christian speech. Ignatius inherited from the primitive church a basic model of belief: Jesus Christ. "You have Jesus Christ in yourselves," he wrote to the church in Magnesia (12.1). Every single word in that sentence went back to the primitive church. By this model, "Jesus Christ," the individual identified himself as a Christian, as a member of the Christian community; it was in Antioch that the name "Christian" had first been given to people believing in Jesus. However, from the very beginning of the Christian movement that model had created divisiveness and had served as a catalyst for personal and social tensions: "it is monstrous to talk of Jesus Christ and to practice Judaism" (Magn. 10.3). It may have been monstrous, but it happened, and it happened long before Ignatius came on the scene. The model that identified the individual and the community was at the same time the cause for dissent and schism, in later epochs even for bloodshed and murder. In what lay the ambiguity and hence the potential for conflict, of such Christian words: "You have Jesus Christ in yourselves"?

That sentence is ambiguous, to begin with, because primitive Christian language models could be used either mythically or historically, and the differentiation between these two usages was not clear nor was it ever understood. A primitive Christian could speak about Jesus Christ mythically; he had at his disposal a wide range of mythopoetic models: God was a heavenly being, the redeemer came down from and returned to heaven. In mythic language a person could certainly say that Jesus Christ was present in man, as a divine force, a heavenly reality. But the Christian could also speak about Christ historically, meaning a person born under Augustus and crucified under Tiberius; yet such a person surely could not be "in yourselves." The ancient Christians seemed to have united the two ways of speaking when they referred to the "risen Lord." But the "risen Lord" belonged to mythic and not to historical language; as Paul realized in 1 Corinthians 1, such language belonged to the realm of the *paradoxon*, hence not to logic and historical verifiability. The dichotomy between mythic and historical, or between mythic and concrete, understanding of Christian models has been an ever-present potential for social conflicts in Christian history; it represented one of the basic dilemmas in the construction of a meaningful Christian belief.

The Christian models were ambiguous because they also vacillated between mythic and metaphysical use of language. They were mythic: Christ was Son, God was Father; but they were also metaphysic: Christ was "word" (*logos*) and "truth" (*aletheia*). God was omniscient and one. As a matter of fact, one and the same model could be used both mythically and metaphysically: God was truth (abstract), and God was Father (mythic); Christ was "faith" (*pistis*—metaphysical), Christ was *logos* (which could be understood abstractly or personally), and Christ was savior (mythic). Why does the ambiguity between mythic and metaphysic understanding of language create problems? Because it matters greatly whether a religious morpheme is used spontaneously as a mythopoetic unit of communication or logically as part of a coherent belief world. If his theological language was mythic, the Christian believer could remain on the level of poetic imagery and affirm belief in a Father and a Son without having to surrender the church's Jewish monotheistic convictions. The myth does not have to have the consistency of a metaphysic, abstract system. If, however, a person used theological language in a metaphysical way, i.e., if he claimed logical coherence within the elements of his belief world, then it became difficult, if not impossible, to maintain two mythic gods by affirming at the same time a monotheistic belief. That conflict between mythic models of belief and the rising demand for metaphysical clarity created the grave theological conflicts of ancient Christianity.

Next, primitive Christian models were ambiguous because they were used simultaneously in an ideological and a social fashion and the two did not coincide. When an ancient Christian spoke about the unity of God, the unity of the church, the oneness of the body of Christ, he experienced and expressed a wish for personal and social unity, a poetic vision of Christian oneness; but even as he spoke or wrote, his social experience contradicted that vision. The Christian church had never been one, not even in its beginnings. Different stories about Christ's resurrection were told, and this first pluralistic evidence, due not merely to the report of different individuals, but to the presence of various Christian groups, became symbolic for Christianity's entire history. The fantasy of Christian unity grew on the soil of constant social discord. The ancient Christian, who applied mythic or ideal images to his communal reality, was not aware—or was only dimly aware at moments of crisis—that he was making claims which were simply not valid or even feasible.

The individual Christian experienced another painful ambiguity, related to the previous one, in the inconsistency between the ethical claims implied in a model and the way he and his fellow believers lived. A Christian was a new being, temple of God, living in Christ. Such terms functioned as an ethical canopy; but they only worked as long as the discrepancy between ideal language and communal reality was repressed; they also worked only as long as there was enough control over relatively small Christian communities so that the variety of ethical behavior, even within the Christian tradition, was not visible. The dichotomy between ethical language and ethical reality contained the potential of sharp conflicts and finally forced patristic Christianity to redefine not only its concepts of baptism and penance, but the very character of the church.

Ambiguity, however, lay not only in the models, mythic as well as metaphysical, organizational as well as ethical, which Ignatius as a member of the Christian church inherited. Ambiguity lay in the very core of the language structure which he took on as a member of the ancient Mediterranean cosmos. What Ignatius had in common with philosophers, priests, merchants, teachers, politicians, and slaves of the ancient world was a vertical-dualistic manner of speaking, containing a number of heterogenous binary particles:

up	and	down
life	and	death
spirit	and	flesh
heaven	and	earth
God	and	man

Within this linguistic framework man communicated with his fellowman, distinguishing what he, or his group, liked, what were his primary values, what he desired, from what he rejected or regarded as inferior. The ancient structure, however, contained at close sight one dilemma after another. "Flesh," to use one of the terms, could be seen, in the most moderate application of the dualistic antithesis, as a force to be dominated by will, as in Stoic ethical writing; in the most extreme use, "flesh" was evil, most pointedly expressed later on by Manichaean groups, or nonexistent, as in Middle or Neoplatonic circles. The dualistic structure permitted a whole scale of sanctions and values, varying not only from one group or person to the next but within the framework of one and the same individual. What factors were responsible for the differences? Both the community and the individuals of such a community. The more a community—think of the Qumran group in its exclusivity—separated itself from the surrounding world, the stronger it applied, to certain issues, the structure dualistically, as for instance in expressing the violent battle of the "sons of light" against the "sons of darkness." The more the individual experienced his isolation from his social context on a given issue —think of Paul's outcries against man's isolation in Romans 7— the more he would use the dualistic structure in a radical way.

However, not only did the vertical structure allow for a wide scale of applications, its different parts arose from different human experiences. Yet, although the different pairs did not speak to the same problem, they were constantly intermingled in everyday speech as well as in the most complicated philosophical writings. The linguistic structure was vertical, I said: heaven was above earth; what was "up" was better; what was "down" was worse. The antique prayer gesture by which hands and arms were raised pleadingly toward the sky expressed the intention well: man hoped that the "better" would come from "above." However, a different kind of experience, of value judgment, was tied in with the vertical cosmological model: the dichotomy between spirit and flesh. Spirit was better than flesh. This model resulted from man's search for a reality behind the phenomena of this world, from a certain contempt for physical existence (*soma sema*). The preference for the spirit over the flesh was construed as consonant with the vertical-cosmological value scheme: the spirit was "above" the flesh. The body was something of a lower order. The assumption of consonance among the vertical terms on each side served well the antique inclinations toward asceticism, purity, mysticism, and salvation, since it gave man's desire to reach an ideal world and to transcend thereby his limited, bodily, earthly existence a cosmic frame.

However, the structure also contained the antithesis between life and death, perhaps the most crucial of its elements. In antiquity, life was "above" and death was "below." God was in heaven, God was absolute spirit, and God was eternal life. The trouble is, life and death are simply not vertical experiences, just as spirit and flesh are not. Furthermore, life, like "spirit" and "heaven," was not merely a term for physical reality, but a symbolic, ideal, hypostatized model with many different meanings, some liturgical, some social, some personal. The ancient linguistic structure consisted, therefore, of heterogenous experiences, a cosmological world view, disdain for the body, fear of death. It is this ancient structure, that was in all its heterogeneity and artificiality extraordinarily effective, which collapsed as the modern world arose with its different cosmic consciousness and its changed attitude toward physical reality.

The maze of models, the ambiguities and plural meanings in ancient man's language do not comprise a single linguistic structure, but an aggregate of patterns, a labyrinth of models, of interconnecting and overlapping elements, drawn from his past as well as from his own human experiences. With this complex and multileveled heritage man creates his event.

IV

At last we come to the document itself. As I have pointed out, this document reflects an *action*. By means of language inherited from his past, within the context in which he lived, Ignatius acted. My task to understand the document is therefore closely connected with my attempt to understand the action, or actions, of which it is the result. The task is a critical one. I experience the remoteness of the document and therefore the reality of historical mutation, I come face-to-face with the precarious connection between words and intent, or between words and social reality, and with the inconsistencies between some words of the documents and others. I feel my way into the action, but I distrust the words. What went on when Ignatius, traveling over the Roman highways and sea routes, wrote down these letters? At the center of my critical task is man's aggressive desire to search out, the wish to lay bare and understand, by breaking through the surface of sentences.

I ask, for instance: Why did the person write the document? Ignatius wrote because people came to see him. They refreshed him, he said (Sm. 9.2), and gave him joy (Magn. 12.1). He wrote as an act of gratitude. But he also needed these visitors; he found in them someone to whom he could say "who he was" (Eph. 12.1). He needed their prayers (Magn. 14.1). But these people were not only support for him; they were also objects. He had found someone whom he could address, control, to whom he could give orders (Magn. 10) and on whom he could enforce, or try to enforce, his monarchical vision of what authority should be (Pol. 6.1). The very first question about the author's motivation gives us access to the social dynamic: What kind of interchange went on as the man wrote, what did he want and need, what role did he play and what role did his visitors play?

The next question concerns the person of the writer, who and what he is. There is a seemingly simple answer: a Syriac prisoner, sent to die in Rome (Eph. 1.1), the martyr for whom "it is better to die than to rule as king over the cosmos" (Rom. 6.1). But he acted precisely like that, like a little king, a bishop over his own little cosmos, the church (Sm. 8. 1–2). But was he really bishop? Why did he need to fight so bitterly in almost every letter for his episcopal theory of government? Surely he would not have stressed obedience so urgently if obedience in the churches had been a matter of fact. But if he was not a monepiscopal leader, why did he act as if he were a bishop?

Then I ask: What was the cause for the action? Why was Ignatius sent to Rome? The letters do not give us sufficient information about the trial and about the events that led to his arrest in Antioch. Clearly he expected to die (Tr. 10.1), and in Rome (Rom. 1.1). But such a sentence was certainly not common, as far as we can tell from the system of Roman provincial administration and legal practice. What happened in Antioch that led to the arrest of Ignatius? The letters do not say. But the letters do say that peace came back after Ignatius was removed from the scene (Sm. 11.2). Did it take Ignatius's arrest and removal to bring peace to the Christians of Antioch? Thinking of the bitter conflicts in apostolic times one is tempted to ask if Ignatius was turned in by foes or if his arrest was related to disturbances either within rival Christian communities or between Christian and Jewish groups.

The veil over the events at Antioch is related to another significant lacuna in these letters. Ignatius did not mention any names in his letters except those of the two people from Antioch who accompanied him and people he met on his journey. He mentioned no one back in Antioch, nor did he mention a single name in Rome. Paul had mentioned many people in Rome. But while Ignatius did not greet anyone in Rome, he knew that there was no bishop in Rome! He nowhere hinted in his letter to the Roman community, a very important community to be sure (*prokathetai*), that his episcopal theory of church government was operating there. The absence of names in these letters and the writer's awareness of the nonexistence of his beloved monepiscopacy in Rome are the most important evidence in favor of the authenticity of these letters. A falsifier could hardly have invented such consistency, and kept such discipline, in regard to names but would have been eager, as was the practice in pseudepigraphal documents, to produce names in order to strengthen the appearance of authenticity of the document. A falsifier in later decades could hardly have known, especially not in the age of Montanism, when bishops belonged to the accepted hierarchy of the church, that at the beginning of the century monepiscopacy was an ecclesiastical system not yet accepted in Rome, but brought into existence by the churches of Asia Minor and Syria. If the letters of Ignatius were a falsification their author would have had to be a Ph.D. in patristics.

To return to my questions: Is it not exceedingly enigmatic that so few names appear in these letters? Was Ignatius very young? Had he been appointed bishop just recently? Was there such an isolation between Antioch and Asia Minor, and between Antioch and Rome, that Ignatius knew no one? But if there had been such isolation, why then did these bishops and presbyters come to see him? Ignatius was eager to imitate Paul (Eph. 12.2); but while Paul always greeted people, Ignatius did not. There are four possible explanations for Ignatius's behavior. Either he was a convert to the Christian church and really knew no one; or he had been made bishop only recently and had lived thus far in anonymity (although this explanation does not suffice to explain the absence of names associated with Antioch); or Ignatius had been bishop of one specific Christian community at Antioch without having the worldwide status which, for instance, Paul had enjoyed among Christians all over the empire; or Ignatius's ability to absorb reality was so limited that he only could face the most immediate social circle.

These critical questions demand an examination of the interaction that took place when each document was written. They suggest that the problems, inconsistencies, and riddles in the texts are due to the fact that the text does not tell the whole story; that the person writing the text hid certain elements, perhaps because he did not want to reveal them, perhaps because he was not fully aware of the problems. In the document, the author may have wanted to play a role and expected his readers to enter into the dynamic by playing roles in response. But words and roles do not necessarily coincide: with the language of love men play war; with the model of submission men play with power. Take the men who came to visit Ignatius, Damas of Magnesia, for instance, who arrived with his presbyters and with his deacon (Magn. 2.1). They came to see a martyr, and Ignatius presented that martyr image to them: he was carrying his bonds around (Magn. 1.2; 12.1). He expressed that image quite vividly to the Ephesians; he was the new Paul, co-initiate with him (Eph. 12.2), the man who gave his life for his people (Eph. 21.1). But many of his visitors did not simply arrive to see a live martyr, they came to visit a bishop. Three of these visitors were bishops themselves, from Ephesus, Magnesia, and Tralles. So was Polycarp, to whom Ignatius wrote his last letter. Since Ignatius's letters emphatically support the episcopal order and since Ignatius obviously tried to strengthen his visitors' hierarchic aspirations (Ignatius loved the deacon Zosimus because of his submissiveness to his superiors [Magn. 2.1]), one must conclude that these bishops came to see him in order to receive support for their own episcopal status (Magn. 7.1). No one would have more weight to strengthen such an ecclesiastical cause than the man who was about to die for his faith. Therefore, the visits of these men were as much a matter of power and control as of devotion and admiration.

Or take the man himself, who wrote to these visitors and their churches. He played the role of the martyr, overcome by danger (Tr. 13.3); the convict (Tr. 3.3). But at the same time, he played the role of the leader (Phil. 7.1). The double attitude can be demonstrated in letter after letter. He did not give the Ephesians any commands, or so he said (Eph. 3.1). But of course he gave them commands, one after another, in chapter after chapter! He was the least of the Christians, he said (Eph. 21.2), unworthy to die (Rom. 9.2), worth so much less than the faithful to whom he wrote (Magn. 11.1). But of course he was worthy (Rom. 2.2), and made so by God's will (Eph. 21.2)! In this dual image of the meek (Pol. 1) and silent leader (Phil. 1.1) and of the authority figure (Magn. 3) fighting for episcopal power as an intrinsic element of Christian life (Sm. 8.1–2), he saw himself as both the outcast (*ectroma* [Rom. 9.2]) and the bishop of Syria (Rom. 2.2), who identified himself with divine authority models, the Father (Tr. 3.1) himself. Just as the visitors came to see Ignatius for both devotion and support, Ignatius appeared to them both as their servant and as their ruler.

The critical questions also demand an examination of the ideological dilemma and of the conflict between different theological and ecclesiological beliefs. Ignatius wrote to his addressees in a highly theological language, using words like "God," "heaven," "Christ," "eucharist," "the new man," "immorality," "eternity." He also employed a mixture of theological and concrete sociological vocabulary: "Where Jesus Christ is, there is the Catholic Church" (Sm. 8.2), and of theological-ethical models that were also tied to the church: "Be zealous to do all things in harmony with God, with the bishop presiding in the place of God" (Magn. 6.1). However, Ignatius also used philosophical ethical speech: "Do not be haughty to slaves!" (Pol. 4.3), "Flee from evil practices!" (5.1). Above all, the theological and philosophical models are constantly in the service of concrete polemic: "Do not be fooled by false teaching and useless old myths" (Magn. 8.1). What do these abstract statements have to do with the event? How does a theological statement function in a concrete situation?

In order to deal with and comprehend the dialectical order of Ignatius's language I isolate units which I call schemata. They are compounds of faith-units; they have at times their own inner logic; they correspond at times to identifiable desires or needs, but they also are, at times, quite irrelevant in relation to the social situation. Sometimes they express a person's experience, sometimes they hide it, i.e., they express the opposite of what a person feels or wants to communicate. The schemata are not independent units, but contemporary structures derived from critical investigation and based upon modern insights into the character of human expression and social interaction.

In the study of Ignatius's linguistic patterns, an obvious starting point is his constant emphasis on unity, what I want to call his "henosis schema." All through his letters are strewn phrases that praise oneness: "There is nothing better than unity," he wrote to Polycarp (1.2). I am not merely speaking about the word "unity" found so frequently in these letters, but about his constant drive to transform traditional images into unity-images and to express "oneness" even when the association of terms was rather far-fetched. He took models he received—"teacher," "eucharist," "prayer," "bread"—and used them for expressing his unity scheme: one teacher (Magn. 9.1), one eucharist (Sm. 8.1), one prayer (Magn. 14.1), one bread (Eph. 20.2). The desire or the need to express unity was primary as Ignatius wrote or dictated his seven letters. The unity drive was not dependent upon any content, upon any image or phrase or topic. It could come with different kinds of models; a unity of ecclesia: one church (Phil. 3.2); a unity of the bishop (Sm. 8); a unity of the liturgical act: break one bread (Eph. 20.2); a unity of theological images, of divine henotes (Eph. 14.1); Christ is one (Eph. 7.2) and God is one (Magn. 7.2). The drive toward unity includes the desire for authoritarian unity in the church (Eph. 2.2) and the poetic hope for a heavenly harmony, the one voice of the heavenly choir (Eph.

4.2). Philadelphians 4 demonstrates the various particles of such a unity drive: Ignatius pleaded for a eucharistic unity around one altar; for a monepiscopal structure with one leading authority figure; for an ideological unity: "There is one flesh of our Lord Jesus Christ."

A critical analysis of such *henosis* passages reveals immediately that the crucial element in them was not the content, the object of unity, but the drive toward unity. What holds the models and phrases in Philadelphians 4 together is the writer's urgent need to find unity. The cause for such need is apparent: the absence of precisely such unity. And indeed, everywhere in these letters are signs of the absence of unity, evidences that the church from which Ignatius came, the churches to which and about which he wrote, were surely not part of a unity. They were divided by doctrines (Magn. 8.1), by practices (Magn. 9.1), by inner discord (Phil. 2.1). It may have been "monstrous" indeed, but it was a fact that "Judaism"—whatever the polemic phrase meant—was practiced in the name of Christianity (Magn. 10.3). The churches were divided by ideological beliefs (Sm. 1–2), as well as by ritualistic practices (Sm. 7).

The threat to unity came from groups that were more related to the Judaistic heritage in the church than Ignatius's own group, but one must be exceedingly cautious before drawing simplistic conclusions about them. Ignatius may have come from a congregation that was considerably removed from the Jewish communities of Antioch. Furthermore, to slander an enemy as a Judaizer (Magn. 8.1) probably worked well, no matter how unfair such an accusation (Phil. 6.1) may in reality have been. Think of Soviet slanders against Yevtushenko as "capitalist" and of American slanders against peace marchers as "communists." Of course, there were anti-Jewish issues, when Ignatius insisted for instance that *Sabbath* be replaced by the *Lord's Day* (Magn. 9.1). But the threat could have come from more than one direction, and the docetic enemies (Sm. 7.1) may, or may not, have been Jewish.

In any case, Ignatius pleaded for the unity of his church, of his community, terrified about the disunited reality of Christianity in Antioch. The church was not one. How much the unity schema in Ignatius resulted from his experience of disunity and from his inability to face disunity can be demonstrated in his use of meta-physical language, for instance in Magnesians 7. Ignatius wrote that "there is one Christ—who came from the Father—who exists toward one and who moved toward one" (7. 2). The phraseology is extremely instructive. Ignatius was not dealing with one but with two models, a Christ model and a Father model. In the very act of writing his words, the duality was apparent and he tried to overcome the awareness that he was actually writing about two models. Three times he tried to bring them together. He *wanted* to bring them together, and he tried in the very act of creating the sentence. Logically it did not work. How can Christ "move toward one" and be "one"; why did he even need to speak about "one Christ" in this context? He tried to fence off the awareness that, at that very moment, he was speaking not about one but about two gods.

The models and phrases with which Ignatius expressed the hoped-for unity of things were not new, of course. Philosophers had for a long time spoken about a principle of unity. So had the writers of Deuteronomy, of Second Isaiah, so had John and Paul, and so had the Roman emperors. What is significant in Ignatius are the intensity of emphasis, the manner in which he combined bureaucratic and theological models, and, above all, the concrete *loci* for the experience of disunity, namely, the emerging but still bitterly contested episcopal power structure and the state of the Christian ideology with its conflicting emphases on monothe-ism and on salvation. The *henosis* schema was the result of a primary social and psychological experience in the life of Ignatius. "It is monstrous to talk of Jesus Christ and to practice Judaism"; one could paraphrase this as follows: "It is monstrous to promise me a secure unity of community and faith and then to let me experience the reality of disunity and schism."

Such a *henosis* schema, as a counterreaction to the pain of dis-unity in the man's thought and in his community, throws light upon important problems which I raised earlier. Churchmen have frequently portrayed Ignatius as the first witness to episcopal authority in the Christian church. The *henosis* pattern indicates a different state of affairs. He was the first who fought desperately, as his letters show, for a monepiscopal structure as a solution to the church's chaos, but that solution was at best merely initiatory. That he did not even mention a bishop in his address to the Romans is significant; in that church which was dearest to him of the churches he addressed he could not even mention a bishop— obviously because he did not know of any, either by name or by his office. The suspicion that Ignatius fought so much for a bishop's power because he did not have such power is confirmed by a remarkable clue in the Letter to the Romans. Asking the Roman church to remember the church in Antioch in its prayers, he stated that Jesus Christ alone looked as bishop (*episkopesei*) over it (Rom. 9.1). He nowhere mentioned a successor; but he did mention Christ as taking his role, as being the subsequent overseer over his former church. It is possible, of course, that Ignatius did not want to acknowledge any successor; but it is also possible that he fell so easily into spiritualizing the act of "overseeing" (*episkopein*) the Antiochian church because he had in his own lifetime not held the full authority which he always wished he had had.

There is a second historical problem connected with the *henosis* schema. Could it be that Ignatius was hiding some crucial facts in regard to his past in Antioch? Are essential clues missing about his capture and condemnation? Ignatius proposed to the Smyrnaeans that they send a delegation to the people of Antioch, congratulating them for their "peace" (Sm. 11.2); he proposed that Philadelphia send a deacon as delegate (Phil. 10.1); and to Polycarp that he call a council and send someone to Antioch (Pol. 7.2). Obviously, Ignatius was desperate to send someone, and he made three separate requests. Why did he want to send a deacon? Why not a bishop? Why no Antiochian names? Why was Christ suddenly the bishop (Rom. 9.1)? Was there a conflict about his episcopal role and was his arrest connected with that conflict? Was he perhaps turned in by rivals? Ignatius talked in his letter in a very impersonal fashion about his former church. A strange thing to do! And why did he not write a letter back to that church? It may have gotten lost. But even in that case, it would be strange that the churches of Asia Minor would have kept his letters while the church that offered the martyr "lost" the letter. I cannot answer these questions because, as I said, crucial clues are absent. But the suspicions are strong enough to warrant a warning against calling Ignatius simply "bishop of Antioch." He may not have been a bishop at all, or at best a shaky one.

I would like to isolate a second basic dimension of linguistic expression and interaction in the letters of Ignatius: the "*thanatos* schema," arising from the life-death dialectic. The letters are permeated with death expectations. Ignatius saw himself as a convict (Tr. 3.3), a condemned man (Eph. 12.1), carrying around his own chains (Eph. 11.2), ready to die (Rom. 6.1). But the mere mentioning of death does not justify the identification of a *thanatos* schema. What makes such passages so significant are their masochistic and mystic connotations. Ignatius said openly that he wanted to suffer (Tr. 4.2), and this longing for pain was so strong that he pleaded to the Roman church not to interfere in his behalf (Rom. 2). A vivid masochistic imagination broke loose as he wrote about that desire: "Rather entice the beasts!" (Rom. 5.2), a fantasy in which he felt physically the final torture of his life. He was to be "ground up by the animals' teeth" (Rom. 4.1). What Ignatius phrased in such sentences was not merely a desire to die but a death wish combined with a longing for physical pain. It would be incredibly naive, after almost a century of psychological and behavioral research, to ignore in such longing for death the man's desire to destroy his body and to eliminate thereby his physical reality. As a matter of fact, in his morbid fantasy, Ignatius did imagine the crushing of his entire body (Rom. 5.3); he had no joy in the "pleasure of this life" (Rom. 7.3); by dying he meant to become man (Rom. 6.2).

The *thanatos* schema includes the antidote to the proximity of death, the models about eternal life (Magn. 1.2). There are various models, and several combinations. "Live according to truth" (Eph. 6.2), "live according to Christ" (Tral. 2.1), "our life" (Magn. 1.2), "our inseparable" (Eph. 3.2) and "true life" (Sm. 4.1). The models include incorruptibility (Rom. 7.3), resurrection (Sm. 7.2), immortality (Eph. 17.1), and the famous medicine of immortality (Eph. 20.2). But also belonging to the schema are the models of the blood (Sm. 1.1) and flesh of Christ (Sm. 7.1) and of the savior (Eph. 1.1). Ignatius does not have one consistent belief in eternal life. He hopes for both resurrection and immortality, and he uses both primitive Christian models, parousia and life with Christ or in Christ, to express this hope. All these models share a common poetic hope in life. It is that poetry which lies at the very center of the early Christian experience.

However, Ignatius's longed-for self-destruction was at the same time a mystic reaching-out for something superhuman, nonhuman. For what? "Pure light" (Rom. 6.2); Jesus Christ (Rom. 6.1); "birth" (Rom. 6.1); "God" (Rom. 6.2). I observe that what Ignatius longed for was not one thing. The language about light and God and birth was a mixture between Hellenistic mysticism and primitive Christian models. But what combined all these metaphors was Ignatius's longing for "something" beyond death. He meant to "attain" a world beyond death, be it Christ or God. How much these two aspects of the *thanatos* schema, the longing for death and the longing for God, were part of the same schema, was expressed by Ignatius in so many words: "with the sword" meant "with God"; to be close to the beasts, to be close to God (Sm. 4.2).

The concrete personal and historical locus of this schema is clear, of course, namely, the immediacy of execution. What is also clear is the psychological implication. Such fantasy about dying reveals a suicidal, self-destructive impulse which is certainly not new with Ignatius, but which he expressed with astonishing candor and vividness. What is much more difficult to assess, however, is the extent of that death wish and the personal dynamic behind it. Historical scholarship finds almost insurmountable walls at such a point: after all, as I pointed out, I cannot interview the man, ask his parents, his peers, talk about his education and the social conflicts during the months and years before his arrest. There are a few observations, however, one can make and from which one can draw certain conclusions, cautious and tentative though they must be. When a person states that by dying he can become a man (Rom. 6.2), and when that statement is juxtaposed to a second one, that in the arena he expected his body to be ground up (Rom. 4.1), finally destroyed (Rom. 5.3), one may ask, from insights learned from contemporary behavioral science, if such hopes indicate an inability of that person to feel that he is a man. A male. To identify as a man. In other words, is the statement that by dying he hoped to become "man" to be taken not as a statement about *anthropos* but about masculine *anthropos*? Is the statement in Romans 6.2 to be taken as a statement about Ignatius's male identity? A second observation seems to me to point in the same direction. Ignatius nowhere comes to terms with the sexual dilemma of his life. Whereas Paul wrote 1 Corinthians 7, and Augustine spent a great part of his literary activity struggling with the problems of fall, concupiscence, and sin, Ignatius almost entirely ignored the problem of sexuality. To be sure, one could say that at the point of facing death, Ignatius had renounced any thought of sexual activity, and that the proximity of death sufficiently explains the omission of that issue. One could also say, however, supported by the various references in his Epistle to the Romans in which he faced death more concretely than elsewhere, that Ignatius's longed-for destruction of his body, of his earthly self, represented a solution to his sexual anxiety, an anxiety which was even greater than among others of the early Christian writers.

Moreover, that we are dealing in Ignatius's death wish with a dream world, with fear and imagination as much as with the actual reality of a legal process and of Roman justice, is strongly suggested as one begins to ask critical questions about his arrest and impending death. Why did Ignatius plead so emphatically that he should be left to die in Rome (Rom. 4.1)? Why did the Roman officials in Antioch send him to Rome in the first place? The Romans would not send a condemned man to Rome unless he were appealing, as did Paul, to the emperor. But if Ignatius had done so, he would hardly have asked the Roman church not to support his plea! If, on the other hand, Ignatius really had been condemned to die in an arena in Rome, shipped from a provincial metropolis—a legal procedure for which, by the way, we have no precedent—then a plea by the Roman Christians, members of a rather despised minority sect, would not have made much difference between A.D. 110 and 115. If Ignatius was a Roman citizen he had the right to appeal; but he surely would not have been sent to die in the arena; and the appeal would have made a reversal possible. If he was not a Roman citizen, one wonders why he was sent to Rome in the first place, and why any plea by the Roman church could make any difference whatsoever. Something does not fit in this historical and legal situation and sequence. My analysis of a *thanatos* schema in Ignatius gives two possible explanations, and each of the two throws light on the problem. Perhaps Ignatius was sent to Rome for trial—perhaps because he asked for it, meaning to replay the life of Paul—and in his expectation of that trial had lost contact with the legal reality, living already in a fantasy world of torture and death. In this case, the plea to the Roman church was a plea to leave him in his somewhat psychotic stage in which he already physically experienced his oncoming destruction. Or Ignatius was indeed condemned to die in a Roman circus—although that would have been unusual in Roman legal practice—and he tried to conquer his fear of death by pleading to the Romans not to interfere. In other words, if he could face death so bravely as even to ask the Romans to remain silent, then such courage, or such seeming courage, could help him tolerate his tragic fate. Both explanations strengthen the observer's feeling that Ignatius on that trip to Rome had lost full contact with the legal reality—which is one of the reasons why it has been impossible for scholarship to solve from his own words the puzzle of his condemnation and of his extradition to Rome.

I isolate a third schema which I want to call the "schema of arcaneness." Ignatius expressed on many different levels and occasions the conviction that he, and the people to whom he wrote, belonged to a special group, separated from the world, distinct from their enemies, with a special theology and a unique ethical behavior: "The person within the sanctuary is pure, the person outside is not" (Tr. 7.2). This schema emphasizes an ecclesiastical uniqueness: the church, famous until eternity (Eph. 8.1), hated by the world (Rom. 3.3), embodies uniqueness in its mystery (Eph. 19.1), its gnosis of God (Eph. 17.2), its belief in resurrection (Sm. 3.1). How ecclesiological and theological arcaneness are intermingled is evident in the sequence: God–Temple–Christ (Eph. 9.2). Exclusiveness is both social and ideological. Christians are "deacons of the mysteries of Christ" (Tr. 2.3). The church is a temple (Magn. 7.2) threatened by the great enemy, the "prince of this world" (Phil. 6.2).

However, the schema of arcaneness has not only two dimensions, ecclesiological and ideological; it contains a further problem because it designated two types of separation. On the one hand, it expresses the separation of the *ecclesia* from the world—God and Christ versus the "prince of this world"—and, on the other hand, the separation of Ignatius's own community from its rivals, from the wicked people, the Judaizers. Ignatius's letters reveal much more the second conflict than the first. The real threat was schism, inner splits (Phil. 3.3); it came from what he called Judaism (Magn. 10) and from what we today call Docetism (Magn. 11).

This arcane schema has implications for our understanding of Ignatius's attitude vis-à-vis Rome. His letters are quite apolitical. The conflict with Rome had not really developed. Arcaneness was therefore primarily sectarian, and the awareness of the presence of a powerful *ecclesia catholica* was certainly not yet present. If Ignatius had been condemned as a result of imperial actions taken against Christians in the wake of Pliny's correspondence with Trajan, or as a by-product of anti-Semitic actions taken by Trajan, he certainly did not reveal any of this. What he struggled for was a clearly defined sectarian congregation. Ignatius was threatened by the prince of this world; his community was threatened by rival sects and rival individuals.

Next I isolate a "schema of monarchic rule." Ignatius sees himself as the bishop (Eph. 4.1) who demands respect (Magn. 3.1) and whom the faithful should fear (Magn. 4), the first in a tripartite authoritarian structure over the church (Sm. 8.1), the monarchic ruler over the faithful (Sm. 8.2). This episcopal role is projected onto God: the bishop is the type of the father (Tr. 3.1), God is bishop (Pol., salutation). But the bishop is also juxtaposed to Christ in that famous analogy of Smyrnaeans 8.2: wherever the bishop appears, let the congregation be present, just as wherever Jesus Christ is, there is the Catholic church. There is not *one* authority model in Ignatius; instead there is a schema by which Ignatius attempts, choosing one model after another, to find analogies, divine, vertical combinations by which to undergird his search for episcopal authority: "united with the bishop" as the church is with Christ, and as Christ is with the Father (Eph. 5); "subject to the bishop" as Christ to the Father and the apostles to Christ (Magn. 13). Christ's relationship to the Father is like the bishop's relationship to Christ (Eph. 3). The schema of monarchic rule contains the passages by which Ignatius speaks about "imitation." He wants imitators of Christ (Eph. 10.3) and of God (Tr. 1.2), and even here he combines the two models: be imitators of Jesus Christ as he was of his Father (Phil. 7.2). Ignatius as bishop identifies with God, the heavenly monarchical ruler; Ignatius as martyr identifies with Christ's death and resurrection.

One of the aspects of the authority schema in Ignatius is his use of control language. Ignatius interspersed his letters with all kinds of exhortative phrases that were pronounced to impose on those arcane communities rules of behavior. The most direct form of such moral control was the command: Let no one be led astray! (Sm. 6.1), Conform! (Magn. 6.2). Another way to enforce behavioral conformity was to say: You see what I desire; you should desire the same! (Rom. 8.1). Or the control was expressed as a threat: If you do not follow such a command, you will not inherit the kingdom of God (Eph. 16.1). The threat as one of the strongest means of force was extended to heaven: Even there judgment will come (Sm. 6.1). Ignatius uses the full force of such threats when he claims that commandments are a matter of life and death (Magn. 5.1). But besides using threats and warnings (Sm. 4.1), Ignatius also controlled his hearers by promising rewards (Phil. 11.2). Such promise of rewards was a form of control, a sophisticated alternative to threats.

The content of such commands was certainly not new. Phrases such as "repent" (Sm. 9.1), "love one another" (Tr. 13.2), "flee wicked practices" (Phil. 6.2), could have been said by many a teacher at Antioch, Jewish as well as pagan. What was new in that schema of monarchic rule was a type of instruction propagating the Christian church's socio-mythic exclusivity: "Live according to *Christianismos*" (Magn. 10.1). What was this *Christianismos*? A unique moral value? Of course not. Christian love did not differ substantially from love propagated by Epictetus or by teachers in a diaspora synagogue. Or what about his admonitions to "flee wicked practices," "flee wicked offshoots" (Tr. 11.1)? Those very phrases were inherited from the Jewish tradition. Teachers from other groups could have warned their members to flee wicked arts. What was "Christian" in Ignatius's schema of monarchic rule was the mythic element in its content and its relation to the arcaneness of the church: To be Christ's temple (Eph. 15.3). That phrase is certainly primitive Christian. However, it did not have any specific moral content that was different from a moral exhortation for purity in Jewish or pagan teaching. Its uniqueness was social, liturgical, and theological. Ignatius, in a way, sensed that difference himself. His ethical admonitions were frequently inserted without much logical connection. They were the least integrated aspect of his literary heritage, thrown in without transition or rational ties: "Abstain from evil plants" (Phil. 3.1), "Love one another with undivided heart" (Tr. 13.2), "Be more diligent, mark the seasons" (Pol. 3.2).

The letter which Ignatius wrote to Polycarp gives us valuable insights into the role and locus of such a language schema. First of all, one is astonished at the amount of exhortative language in that letter. Polycarp surely needed such constant moral hammering less than all the other addressees of Ignatius in Philadelphia or Tralles, if Ignatius believed his own description of him as being "godlike in mind" (Pol. 1.1). Then why so much moralizing in the Polycarp letter and so little in the one to the Romans? A clear indication that Ignatius's preoccupation was not so much with the addressees as with himself! The prima facie inconsistency dissolves the moment one understands how this man's language operated. He did not write to the Romans simply in order to exhort them, but in order to work through his fear of death and to prepare himself for his arrival in Rome; he did not write to Polycarp to tell him he should "be good" but in order to identify with him. Polycarp was his episcopal ideal, young, promising. What was going on between Ignatius and the Romans was not at all the same as that between Ignatius and Polycarp. One phrase really proves my point. In writing to Polycarp, Ignatius told him: "Give heed to the bishop that God may give heed to you" (Pol. 6.1). Now Polycarp was the last man who needed to hear such words, because he *was* a bishop! Why then did Ignatius write a sentence of that kind to him? Because he wrote it, in a way, to Polycarp's people, and he said it not to Polycarp but, in fact, in Polycarp's place. He identified, as he wrote his letter, with Polycarp as a bishop and repeated that familiar phrase as if to strengthen his own position and as if to speak to his own people. The same projection occurred in his many other exhortative phrases in the Polycarp letter. When he wrote such sentences as "Not all wounds are healed by the same plaster" (2.1), "Be prudent as the serpent" (2.2), "Be sober as God's athlete" (2.3), he identified with Polycarp as teacher and spoke to Polycarp's, or his own, listeners. In a way, he was the teacher-bishop again, back in Antioch, instructing the church by models and modes which he had in common with the antique rhetorician as well as with the rabbi, apostle, or bishop of Judaeo-Christian Syria.

The fifth schema is that of "historical recital." Twice in his letters, in Smyrnaeans 1 and Trallians 9, Ignatius paraphrased an early Christian creed, the birth, death and resurrection of Jesus Christ in poetic-hymnic concentration. Many references to that creed appear throughout the letters: birth and baptism (Eph. 18.2), suffering (Sm. 7.1), passion (Sm. 12.2), cross (Eph. 9.1), death and resurrection (Magn. 11.1). The locus of this schema was the liturgy of the congregation. The creed was not Ignatius's own fabrication, it was part of the liturgical tradition of the church, asyndetic poetry as hymnic celebration. What happened when Ignatius transferred and used this creed or elements thereof in his letters? He quoted. He remembered. The community had quoted and remembered. To be sure, when Ignatius quoted or paraphrased the creed, the liturgical locus was replaced by a polemical one. When Ignatius added to Trallians 9 the words: "He both ate and drank," he demonstrated the polemical function of the creed. In the schema of historical recital, the member of the Christian community also put himself into a historical sequence. The mentioning of Pontius Pilate and Herod the Tetrarch in Smyrnaeans 1 established, or recalled, a point in history.

The schema of historical recital was built on an explosive contradiction: it was mythic and historical at the same time. The basic stories of the Pentateuch had contained such ambivalence, to be sure. Abraham and Moses were mythic as well as historical phenomena. But man no longer experienced the two kinds of models naively but had begun to deal with the discrepancies, in Greek as well as in Jewish tradition. Ignatius did not see the problem. As a matter of fact, he was totally uncritical about "history," and the modern historian would have to say there was no real history in his thought. Furthermore, the process of mythic-historical recital led to a totally personalized, self-absorbed understanding of the creed. Ignatius was actually suffering, *he* was crucified, *he* was dying. *He* identified with the risen Lord.

Nevertheless, in such historical recital, no matter how mythic and how fragmentary it appears in this primitive Christian document, the kernel of an emerging historical Christian consciousness was present. Here was the *memoria*, the perspective, no matter how fragmentary, which distinguished the ancient Christian community from Isis, Persephone, and Mithra and brought the Christian church into political confrontation with *divus imperator*—in whose historical recital mythic and historical phenomena were similarly interwoven. Not long after Ignatius's death the Christian bishops began to trace their succession to their historical-mythic point of departure, like the Roman emperors of the second century.

The last unit is the "schema of mythic projection." As was typical for a man in antiquity, Ignatius received a vast amount of mythic imagery and along with it inherited many different ways of using these mythic images. These images justified his personal agony, they served as objectifications for his fears, they permitted him to play and to let his imagination flow, they served his social aspirations, they gave him a framework in which to function. In some of these images, his personal experiences are explicit; others served to hide his inner life. To many an observer, the mythic schema should be subsumed in the preceding schemata, because the mythic projection always serves either a social or a psychological function. I do not agree with such extreme reductionism. The mythic enterprise, so basic to ancient man, represents a world in itself, a play in its own right. It is related, of course, to all the other schemata I suggested, and I have made it clear by now that these schemata do not function independently but frequently overlap with each other. The mythic activity of the ancient world is a phenomenon which in itself created important historical movements and produced religious, artistic, and philosophical momentum. Important in this phenomenon is its multileveled character. At times some elements of the mythic belief world are directly related to social and personal experiences, at times they are not at all. There is no consistent relevance, no consistent locus, and yet originally each model had such relevance and such a locus. Only when I begin to analyze the contradictions and patterns of the mythic belief worlds can I identify where, if at all, mythic memory is related to concrete experiences and even events, where it is employed to create new mythic sequences by which the individual or the church creates a new ideological framework within which to function, and where it is poetic recall without social or personal implications.

Because mythic texts contain so many strata, I must divide this schema into different patterns. Otherwise I risk creating the impression that dealing with myth is a uniform and simple process; in reality the myth combines several patterns. During Ignatius's era, mythic language was already in process of being transformed into or juxtaposed to metaphysic language. The two are related to each other in that they are both products of human objectivizing; but the transformation from one to the other represents a crucial change in mental activity. When man began to create metaphysical instead of mythic images, he had to become more conscious of life and he experienced, often with enormous inner conflicts, the quickening of his rational abilities. The change involved not only a critical awakening but a limitation of the poetic character of theological and philosophical speech. Hence the crisis, since poetry cannot be replaced by philosophy without man's losing primal emotional forces. And a nonmythic poetry was obviously not a live option for the ancient church. Were I dealing with a later epoch of history, I would have either to add a seventh schema, that of creating abstract ideas, or replace the schema of projection with one of abstraction. In the patristic church the mythic and the metaphysical activity were so intimately related that they cannot be separated. It is that intertwinement which is responsible for much fascinating theological dynamic. When theologians understood "Son" and "Christ" as *logos* models, they were performing the transformation of mythic into metaphysical language. They had advanced too far along the way to historical consciousness to accept naively the world of mythic images, yet they could not give up the poetic-mythic elements of their heritage—"Jesus Christ is the Lord." Nor could they help analyzing the myth; they were compelled to ask questions about the logical content of their myths: If Christ is Lord, do we have two gods? The theologians of ancient Christianity vacillated, often in the course of a single sentence, between mythic and metaphysical language play.

I distinguish three patterns by which Ignatius dealt with his mythic traditions. The first is "the pattern of antithesis." Ignatius, heir to conventional Near Eastern parallel language structure (faith and love, Sm. 13.2), pitched a positive model against a negative one and thereby created a value distinction related to his personal agony and fear and to the social conflicts in which he was involved. The antithesis was a cosmic one: God versus cosmos (Magn. 5.2), God versus flesh (Rom. 8.2): in the cosmos the abolition of death was planned (Eph. 19.3). The antithesis contained the alternatives of "death" (*thanatos*) and "life" (*zoe*) which were, as many of the other components, metaphysical as well as mythic, hypostatized models: life versus death (Magn. 5.1), life versus passion (Magn. 5.2), resurrection versus death (Tr. 9.2). Both the negative and the positive components were interchangeable; the negative ones were the world (Rom. 7.1): flesh (Magn. 6.2), *eros* (Rom. 7.2), *hyle* (Rom. 6.2), the positive ones were God (Rom. 8.2), Christ (Rom. 5.3), immortality (Magn. 6.2), resurrection (Tr. 9.2), life (Magn. 5.1). In the inscription of the letter to the Philadelphians he juxtaposed first "passion" with "resurrection" and then "blood of Christ" with "external and remaining joy." Faithful to antique vertical structures of value, the positive was the higher, and the relationship between the lower and the higher was one of subordination: the Father of Jesus Christ was the bishop of all (Magn. 3.1).

The pattern of mythic antithesis has personal as well as social significance for Ignatius, but while the social function was unambiguous the personal was not. In regard to his own personal, inner experiences, Ignatius identified at times with the positive, higher components: "Be on my side, which is God's side" (Rom. 7.1), he wrote at one time quite bluntly. But such identification was, of course, only part of his experience. He experienced the opposite: he *desired* to identify with the positive (Rom. 8.1) and he asked the Romans to pray for him so he might reach it (Rom. 8.3). In regard to the social significance, Ignatius showed no ambiguity about his mythic antithesis. The death–life antithesis (Magn. 5.1) was juxtaposed by the image of two coinages, and these two coinages represent God and the world (Magn. 5.2). What do these two coinages really mean? The believer and the unbeliever (Magn. 5.2). The life–death alternative with which Ignatius began and terminated his case in Magnesians 5 was tied in with his communal conflicts. But in that conflict, Ignatius was entirely on the side of God.

Mythic antithesis, however, also leads to poetic descriptions of the cosmic drama of redemption in which the dualistic components are no longer predominant. In Ephesians 7 Ignatius created a poetic vision of life's duality, intuitive, ambivalent, suggestive not only of the tragic in life's experiences, but also of the positive dimension in its dialectic. Later dogmatic observers tried to force these statements into the procrustean bed of christological agreements whereas they were in fact a spontaneous creation in Ignatius's search for life:

one physician	
both of flesh	and of spirit
born	and unborn
God	in Man
in death	true life
of Mary	and of God
passible	impassible
Jesus Christ	our Lord.

Eph. 7

There is a second pattern, less part of the general heritage of antiquity, although important roots and parallels can be found in both Jewish Wisdom Literature and philosophic speculations. This is the "pattern of stratified god languages." The ancient Christian church, even in New Testament times, had begun to operate with two, and then with three, distinct and yet frequently confused god languages. It is methodologically futile to try to determine if Ignatius believed in one god or two gods, if his theology was subordinatory or modalistic, to use later terms. The problem cannot be posed in that way. Ignatius had three god languages, and each of them had its own logic and each had its own contradictions vis-à-vis the others. The first god language was monotheistic. Different from the case in other patristic writers this first god language was not a major factor in his theological scheme. But he clearly believed in the power of God the Father (Magn. 3.1) and spoke about "attaining to God" (Rom. 9.2), as if the basic pattern of theological thinking was the relation between God and man. Ignatius had a second god language, that of the "Son," of Christ (Eph. 20.2). The second was God, too, the "God Jesus Christ" (Eph. 18.2). In this theological pattern, Ignatius could speak about "attaining to Christ" (Rom. 5.3), as if the basic relationship were between Christ and man. At times, therefore, Ignatius operated with a Father-God language and at times with a Son-God language. He confused the two frequently, of course. In retrospect it is quite difficult to determine when *kyrios* applied to the first and when it belonged to the second. He switched from one to the other, he tried to combine the two—"by the will of the Father and Jesus Christ our God" (Eph., salutation) —and he often operated as if only the second existed (Eph. 7). The two god languages have their own specific logic and their own locus. The monotheistic Father-God language belongs to the Jewish tradition, although it could also arise in Greek philosophical circles related to the Jewish past (cf. the pseudo-Aristotelian *De Mundo*), its psychological locus was the need for unity; its political dynamic was the claim for a unified world under one's own autocratic vision. The Son-God language belonged to the primitive Christian experience of Jesus Christ as savior; its locus was the church, the community, the liturgy; its psychological dynamic was rooted in the need for a mediator. Ignatius had inherited a third god language, trinitarian or rather, at this time of the patristic evolution, triadic. The Holy Spirit was a rope, a pulley (Eph. 9.1). The third god language was not very well developed in Ignatius. Its locus was the liturgy. Three-god models required a different logic from that required by two-god models, or even by the one-god model. To isolate and analyze three god languages for the ancient church—rather than to disentangle insoluble monotheistic-christological problems by later trinitarian categories which in themselves are at best full of inner contradictions—opens the study of the ancient church in a new way, and there could hardly be a better example for the advantages of such an approach than Ignatius of Antioch. Scholars as well as theologians of the ancient church have often wondered about such distinctions between the concepts God and Christ. With the proposition of juxtaposed, stratified god languages I do not have to answer the insoluble question of whether he believed in one god or in two. At times he operated with one type of god language and sometimes with the others. The task of the patristic theologians consisted in trying to resolve the differences between Ignatius's and his church's several god languages, and to reconcile the differences between the logical and the existential dimensions of their belief worlds.

The problem posed by such juxtaposition of god languages was not Ignatius's alone, of course. It belonged to the mythological crisis of the ancient world. Long before Ignatius, the mythic and tribal gods began to be demythologized, e.g., they were replaced by abstractions, by "one God," by one principle. They were "understood." But that principle of unity did not explain life sufficiently—Plato had already seen the problem; or it did not, as Job, the Wisdom Literature and the Middle Platonist philosophers pointed out, explain the problem of evil, man's anxiety, and his feeling of alienation in the world. Either the syncretistic threats to religion were too great, or the social and psychological disunity was too intense; in either case, a second god language or principle language was introduced, a language structure that posited a second god distinct from the first. Actually Philo did say in so many words: *deuteros theos*. Models of emanation, of a *demiourgos*, of an agent of creation, a divine *logos*, an intermediary, a redeemer were put next to the one principle, the One God who then became more and more transcendent. The vertical stratification marked the character of late antique religious and philosophical thought. What was the locus of such vertical stratification of god languages? The syncretistic cities of the Greek and Graeco-Roman cosmos, the schools, religious groups, and sects whose leaders sensed the collapse of both the traditional mythic structures and the monistic principles that had emerged as a first reaction to that collapse.

At rare moments, Ignatius created a cosmic drama. I call that enterprise the "pattern of cosmic play," the most beautiful exam-

ple of which is Ephesians 19. The prince of this world did not
know anything about the great mysteries of the cosmos. A star
shone. There was a cosmic dance, perplexity, newness. The drama
of destruction began, the old kingdom was destroyed, abolition of
death was planned. The individual elements of this vision were
not new, of course. With them, however, Ignatius created his
poetic vision, a counteraction to his experiences, a projection of
social conflicts, in a language event that was itself experienced as
drama. In chains Ignatius sang (Magn. 1.2); in expectation of death
he heard a choir sing (Rom. 2.2). Such images were themselves
celebrations, mimeses of hope. The pattern of cosmic play, to be
sure, had its locus, originally, in the liturgy where the community
played and experienced freedom and deliverance in their participation in the drama. But the cosmological passage of Ephesians
19 was the individual's emergence into creativity, into poetic and
dramatic play. Here the martyr became an artist who created his
own epics out of the mythic fragments of his heritage. Ignatius
offered to his tortured readers, who like him had lost their social
and personal roots, the poetic vision as antidote to the terror of life.

These are the important linguistic schemata that can be identified in the letters of Ignatius. What have I gained by analyzing the
document in such a way? In the first place, I have found important
clues to the answers to historical questions that have been posed
time and again. The methodology has made clear how divided was
the church from which Ignatius came, how tenuous was his episcopal role, and what serious questions must be raised about his
arrest and condemnation.

In the second place, I have recognized the ambiguity of the man,
Ignatius. There are some clear patterns behind his inconsistencies.
Each of the schemata analyzed contains its own ambiguities, and
these ambiguities account for many of the historical and theological problems. Ignatius said, for instance: "I do not give you commands" (Eph. 3.1); but he gave one command after another. He
praised the Ephesians for having no heresy among them (6.2);
but then he warned them all the time against heresy (7.1; 9.1).
These ambiguities have shown how carefully the seemingly clear
and straightforward propositions must be handled in historical

research. The church of Ephesus was threatened by heresy right and left, of course. And it is indeed open to doubt if Ignatius was an acknowledged bishop or if he was only trying to play this role and in his attempt was betrayed, or perhaps even failed.

In the third place, this approach concretely opens up Ignatius's multileveled reality, the plurality of his belief worlds. Man lives on several levels. Once pluralism is understood, one does not need to create, in retrospect, an artificially synthesized "theology" or "ethic." The schemata are a tool to understand the relationship between theological language and social realities, between Ignatius's letters and the context in which he wrote his letters. It shows how many factors could operate in his faith as well as in his life, and on how many levels he could act and interact, as poet, as leader, as martyr.

In the fourth place, I have been able to show with concrete examples that words do not possess any given absolute meaning but belong to functional structures in which the words themselves are frequently interchangeable. In most cases, the words and the schemata were not identical. The word "God," for instance, appeared in different schemata; it served as a model of power, it helped Ignatius pronounce control over the churches in affirming his episcopal theory, it belonged to the schemata of arcaneness, of historical recital, and of cosmic projection. It is only its context which determines the meaning and value of a word.

In the fifth place, the schemata have shown that what is unique to Ignatius's language are not specific words but the combinations of words; not models but mosaics of models. In the combination and function of models we receive a glimpse of the writer's dynamic, of his polemic, his fears and aspirations. In the way a writer repeats or emphasizes models one can find out which issues were primary in given situations.

These schemata have laid out the turmoil of Ignatius's life. His church was not one; he could not face the legal reality of his trial; he was terrified to die; he believed in God and Christ; he wanted to be bishop very badly. In these relationships between images and social reality we catch a glimpse of the drama of ancient Christianity. Because his images did not fit, the ancient Christian individual took on himself the task of finding new images and combinations, the creative process of searching for new combinations; because the church was not one, the bishop fought for unity; because life was, at heart, unbearable to the man from Antioch, he sang and heard a choir sing.

V

Man not only shares in history, he creates it. The historical encounter does not end with the analysis of the specific historical event or events. That event must be understood not only in its origins and in its concretion but in its relation to what happens afterwards; it exists in a continuum, not a linear continuum, to be sure, but one of irregular motions and tortuous convolutions. The continuum extends to our very present, and it is that continuum, no matter how complex and multileveled, which makes it possible that the original document can be understood at all. In the fifth step I examine Ignatius's contribution to the future. This task involves offering interpretative explanations in larger contexts, and leads back to the present, to the hermeneutic problematic with which I began this essay. The event at Smyrna cannot be separated from events that followed it because that event contributed to creating what followed in the twentieth, as well as in the second century. The scope of this essay allows for a few hints only, about what the interpretative enterprise must consider, in relation to three problems: monepiscopacy, martyrdom, and Gnosticism.

Monepiscopacy. Ignatius was not bishop of Antioch; but he felt the trend of the times, realizing the need to establish a monarchical authority structure in order to lead the church out of the inner chaos with all its rivalry and insecurity. The struggle for monepiscopal power in Ignatius was prophetic—and on that count the man who was about to die had proved to be a seer. By the middle of the second century, monepiscopacy began to transform the church; by the middle of the third century, it had won the day: for Cyprian, "Where the bishop is, there is the church" (*ubi episcopus, ibi ecclesia*). However, by the middle of the fourth century, a metropolitan structure had assumed great power, and by the middle of the fifth century, the monepiscopal idea was in clear competition with a powerful patriarchal-papal authority structure. Ignatius contributed to shaping organizational structures; but he also pointed to the dilemma about the justification of such authority. He did not justify his authoritarian vision by any legal argument based on election or succession. The episcopal power was simply based on the fact that he said it, that he personified it. At times he saw himself, his life—and therefore his personal power—as parallel to that of the apostles, at times as parallel to Christ's, at times even to God's. Ignatius had the power because he wanted power, because he believed he had a right to be bishop. The roots of such power are both personal, emanating from the drive for personal leadership, and cultural, arising from antique political and social forms of state and society. Since the monepiscopal idea was a historical phenomenon, depending upon the interplay between Ignatius's needs and his culture, that monepiscopal structure was doomed to collapse if ever the political and social structures of the culture were substantially altered. With the coming of the Renaissance, with the emerging Protestant democratic societies, and finally with the *aggiornamento* of the Roman Catholic political and social framework, the Ignatian monepiscopacy, that mixture of paternalistic sublimation and wise adaptation of antique administrative leadership, could not survive the cultural transformations of the modern world. The traditional bishop, whether in the person of Cyprian, Cranmer, Boniface VIII, or Pius IX, no longer presents a viable option of authority in a democratic society. The analysis of Ignatius's episcopal language showed how much in its very emergence the monepiscopal ideal was a precarious mixture of imperial-antique political and communal reality and a Christian's fantasy world.

Martyrdom. To understand a specific phenomenon it helps to see it going off *post festum* in several directions. Because of the potentially political character of Ignatius's ecclesiastical dynamic, his image of martyrdom could become incendiary. It did. By the end of the century, the martyr had become a rebel against Rome. The acts of the Scillitan martyrs show strong political overtones. So do the trial acts of Crispina. On the other hand, the leadership of the church tried to reduce the socially irresponsible elements in martyrdom by emphasizing that only when God induced martyrdom should it be undergone. In other words: we don't want too many martyrs! Such restriction was meant to arrest the self-destructive impulses inherent in martyr ideology, all the while retaining the political value of having some members undergo the ordeal of martyrdom. After the martyr had helped the Christian elite to reach victory over the pagan powers, the next stage was to make out of the martyr an apolitical ideal with which the Christian could be led to submission. The martyr was transformed from the avant-garde Christian to the fairy-tale figure, the miracle worker. However, even then the "martyr" became a strong reality again, not as a person, to be sure, but as an abstract language model of control and teaching: look at such a Christian and you will be stronger yourself! The martyr became a model to justify suffering: see how much more these people had to suffer in their lives, and stop complaining about your suffering which is so much less than the cruelties and horrors they had to endure! The ideal which Ignatius had put up for himself became, strangely enough, an ideal with which his episcopal successors quite successfully operated later. The martyr became the hero of the past, and as such a hero he became an important model for literature as well as for art. In the modern world the martyr is no longer a divine hero. The moment we look at Ignatius not only through the vision of the *legenda aurea*, but of *Androcles and the Lion*, the death wish of Ignatius ceases to function as a dream about a heroic future.

Gnosticism. The problem must be divided into specific issues. On the communal level, Ignatius represented a special autocratic trend in the church which led to Irenaeus and Cyprian and not to Valentinus and Basilides. On the level of symbolic language—ritual and historical recital—Ignatius represented a trend that did not lead to the Docetism of the apocryphal gospels but to ecclesiastical catholic developments; the medicine of immortality (Eph. 20.2) became transubstantiation and not Valentinian symbolism. On the level of mythic projection, Ignatius did have dualistic patterns and he did create cosmological poetry. But his dualism was rather a far cry from the antitheses in the emanative systems of the second century. If one calls the late antique objectifications, as Hans Jonas has done, "Gnostic," and includes in such a schema the entire development from Philo to Plotinus, Ignatius of course belongs to that development. If belief in a redeemer-god is by definition Gnostic, Ignatius is Gnostic. But if one restricts, as I believe one has to, in order to talk meaningfully about Gnosticism at all, the Gnostic phenomena to second century emanative dualism, then Ignatius has at most merely some elements which belonged to traditions that led to Gnosticism. He did not have, for instance, the sexual inversion so prevalent in Gnostic texts (*probole, nymphoma, syzygia*, begetting, the bisexuality in the Gospel of Thomas, the male-female dialectic in the primal Gnostic images), nor did he believe in the spiritualization of *ecclesia*, so symptomatic for Gnostic approaches to society. When the drive toward unity embodied the episcopal autocracy and the external structure of the church, no matter how much the hope was part of fantasy and death wish, we are not dealing with Gnosticism but with the phenomenon of an emerging socio-political movement, the Catholic church.

Such is the fifth step, which cannot encompass the entire historical continuum, but must be strictly limited to given issues and to the most essential observations. To deal with the material in terms of its subsequent history and in relation to and in distinction from our present age forces the observer to make interpretive choices—and without such choices, no matter how complex and risky they turn out to be, the historical enterprise is not only incomplete, it is dull, misleading, and incapable of dealing with history, i.e., with life, significantly. It is the analysis of such subsequent histories of a document that reveals its incompleteness, that fragmentary character of the human record which I predicated at the outset and which my type of analytic investigation so clearly reveals.

The letters of Ignatius are fragments not only because they represent a quantitatively small body of evidence, written down during moments of intense excitement, but because all language is limited and all data are mere fragments. The historical evidence is "open," is unfinished because life is open, is unfinished. I cannot act as if the historical datum were something different from my own life. When I write a poem and read it and when the hearer receives it and passes it on, the poem goes through transformations. It can be read and heard on many levels, and its character is changed by the insights and experiences of the hearers. Historical evidence is not an exact parallel to artistic datum, because it contains precise data that do not change, names, numbers, the fact, for instance, that Ignatius wrote in Ephesus in Greek, called himself *Theo-phoros*, etc. When I call the historical document "unfinished" I mean that *certain* factors are *always* new, and that hence the totality of the datum remains open. I must always ask again what happened, how can I understand the evidence, the man, his actions? But even my question changes the character of the document. When I say the historical document is unfinished, I do not "finish" it by merely relating it to the present. On the contrary, it is exactly in knowing the "open" character of both the language of the document and my own life that I experience the dynamic of historical evolution, the process of mutation. To the person who has gone to history as a substitute for metaphysics, such insights may be quite threatening. At the recent annual meeting of the American Historical Society, one of the historians lamented the fact that historiography has become terribly fluid and is no longer the clearly defined discipline it used to be. Indeed it is not. The process of life, our age has taught us, is not safe and clearly defined. Ignatius's letters are open documents both in relation to his own life and to that of contemporary man.

I am not only aware of and I not only acknowledge consciously the "unfinished" state of the evidence, but I am also aware of the element of play in the historical enterprise. The analysis of the document is, among other things, an experiment in creativity and creativity is play. To acknowledge the element of play in historical work strikes many academicians as a dangerous or even inadmissable adulteration of scholarship. It can justify abuses and bigotry as well as dilettantist work. But in fact such playing has clear rules: those of historical inquiry ("What can actually be documented?" and "What can we find out?") and those of rational discourse ("What can I say?" and "What can I conclude?" and "How can I safeguard my assumptions?"). Limits here, as in any other play, do not destroy it, but represent the structure within which it becomes possible. "Play" has a pejorative connotation in academic work as in a puritan society. But this negative attitude does not change the fact that the historian at his best is *homo ludens*, man enjoying himself in the exercise of his creativity. I cannot define "play," I can only play it. The encounter with Ignatius is play because it invokes and nourishes my imagination; because it leads me into a mimetic attempt at the artistic re-creation of human emotions and actions; because it tries to recapture the drama in the life experiences, both tragic and comic, of human beings who lived in times and places remote from ours. It is play because it is unpredictable. It is play because I love to do it. The historian engages in this "play" in order to comprehend, but more than that such play is the creative expression of his own many faces and moods: the historian can be iconoclast, poet, scientist, humanist, with freedom to laugh or to curse darkness. It has always been so, though many historians exercise this aspect of their creativity furtively. The greatest of the historians, how-ever, from Gibbons to Ranke to Lietzmann and Morison, have always been able to give rein in their work to the element of play.

The five steps which I have outlined and the methods which I have employed do not represent one tightly knit methodology, but various options, stages and possibilities. I am fully aware that I have not solved the twofold problematic of contemporary histori-cal research, namely the conflict between past and present and the tensions among multiple research perspectives. Options are related to particular experiences and insights. To show what kind of options my methodology is free to choose, I offer as my second contribution to this book one of a series which I call *Juxtaposi-tions*. Like everything in my work, it is experiment, interpretation as well as response. It has its own form and its own freedom. Just as in drama and poetry the old logical categories of chronological sequence and causal connections have been replaced in favor of a new poetic logic, which admits as its starting points an ambiguity consonant with the mixed character of life, so my story on Abra-ham and Isaac has its own inner structure, a logic of juxtaposition, expressing its meaning in a paradox interplay of images. Shortly before his death I had lunch with Paul Tillich on the Quadrangle Club, and he commented on my work. "You have your demons," he said, "as I have mine. Demons drive us, perhaps, out of the sanctuary; they make us into gatekeepers, or they just send us straying. But one thing demons do which nobody can. . . ." And he looked over the table, the German eighty-year-old thinker who had come from the battlefield of depressed Germany in the twenties to the liberal milieu of the University of Chicago in the sixties: "They take you to the *Grenzerlebnis,* and don't you let anyone hold you back from that." It is that experience of the border, the search for meaning at the limits of possibilities which I try to push toward in the following pages.

SAMUEL LAEUCHLI

abraham and isaac

nightmares and window panes
in my waking up
analogy of disbelief
by which i grasp the doom
of my tilted globe

it is quite a dream to wake into
isaac outstretched for murder
a slaughter knife in the hand of abraham
voices ringing with orders
sacrifice him
don't
love him
don't kill him

in the intense debate as to which symbolic forms are still
possible and whether or not we are capable still of living
in symbolic realities i am not sure where i come out since
my entire life has been one constant struggle in my raging
body
erase what has been wrought
recall what you have buried
events scratch their marks into my memory and memory means
nerve endings that sting in me desperate desires to forget
the pain which burnt its scars into my living cells
what makes my fantasies so horrible i didn't make them up
when faced with my forgetting i feel my anger rise at dawn
my memory turns nightmare counting
innocent
unbelievers
sacrificed
piled up
isaac stretched out for murder
on the holy mountain where the nights refuse to redeem

my memory is window panes through which to
watch into distance
replayed
caves of lascaux
reversed recalled
so i can go on again and love and not destroy
let my future begin
back at lascaux where
waking up began
harts symbols bison signs taurus color texture male female
darkness memory future
ochre green yellow red black ochre red red
dyed tears on the walls
not only my own
waking up tears laughing at waking up tears
sealed bloodshed on the walls
the only seal i have to go to lascaux with is my own blood
my father's
to write
my history
with the silence of my longing

my story begins about forty years ago in a new york flat
three people around a table the man the woman the boy
trinitarian model of sorts and caravaggio in composition
the man aristocratic southern enormously successful at
hand rolled cigars enormously successful with women
immaculately dressed rich immaculately shaved rich
the rugs and the crystals and the curtains one grandiose
extension of the patriarch's apeneck hirsute body

the woman drab sweet intelligent gentle
complicit posture of insured domesticity

her dress
cut
not to display
the loveable round shapes with which he
dared at times
to fondle before médoc was uncorked
for the châteaubriand with bernaise

her fingernails pink light pink
cruel pink since pink can be more cruel
than most other fingernail polishes

the boy
yes the boy
i don't really have images to introduce the boy
adolescent about that monstrosity which we call life
terrified that abraham might take him on a hideous journey
wanted to love and to be loved
like every one of us
how cheap it sounds in retrospect
and the mind of the boy was opaque

sunday dinner and the afternoon sun broke into
windows
the man in need of brisk air and the woman
constantly on the shivering point
they arranged for a compromise between the spicy
autumn wind and the wintry steam rushing
through the radiators and left the windows a slit open
which made no one secure
but brought temporary truce for a compromise celebration

they celebrated by
recalling celebrations
the day they went for rides and the city was so much more
humane than now riverside a parkway of joy and i took you
on sunday afternoon in a buggy and you loved it

you were happy
darling happy
no jams under polluted skylines with mafia bribed cops no
teenage gangs tourists blackouts jewish negro warfare
rocks of manhattan
remember the soloists in our little church
how beautiful
upon the mountains
and the voices of the priests did not ring with doubt

how the wind cracked the windows
into freedom
and the boy sat quietly and would have loved to try
the sparkling rosé in the heavy crystal

we feasted in one of old manhattan's swankiest taverns
snails and calf brains
don't call me barbaric
you loved the snails and we had rosé
remember lancers the first time you had lancers since
your parents knew no wine
we drank to snails and lancers and your parents'
wedding night
a toast to innocence
remember the afternoon i wanted to lay you on the lawn
bushes thick with smell
a toast to mediterranean sunshine
spirea honeysuckle you screamed it was a riot
a month before king james and lohengrin and all that
you wouldn't let me pull your panties down
fought back bit kissed scratched kissed fought to the end
remember the lush fragrant blossoms above half nude bodies

that night i invited you to the opera and we made up
cocoa and muffins good muffins hot
steaming cocoa it felt so good
traviata and you wept all night in my bed

i told you it didn't matter what happened to violetta
and esthetics was at heart amoral and hence
irrelevant to our social dynamic
if it hadn't been isaac it would have been someone else
my anger was silent and my hands could not be still

the boy doesn't know what he's in for

why did it happen
sometimes we need catharsis and our own children
must be the witnesses
he who recalls may forgive
longer than he who forgets
it takes them a lifetime nonetheless to pay for
having been the witnesses for our doom
they'd have to pay just the same for having gone bowling

why did i lose my mind that afternoon
spirea and the spite of the boy
he hated me
woman cries in panic don't use that word not once again
but he did and you did
innocent woman
i feel the word crawl down my throat

remember the afternoon with autumn falling leaves
ochre brownish orange yellow
old new york played with its sugar maples
how can they let our city collapse in its own shell
i wish i could remember
can't you tell me
why is man
insane

it's quite a day when a child
learns about his parents' insanity

walks over to the window
here
look here boy
woman look here
the window's open
so you can hear the insane cries of a child

the boy
held
by his left leg
look down
thirteen stories

daddy it's not thirteen stories down you must mean
the other house we live only on the seventh floor

the boy
held by his left leg
he screamed the woman screamed
abraham's knife ready for the killing
boy can't you hear yourself scream
you damn fool how could you forget what i did to you

don't scream again it's too late
i didn't do it
just held you
as if
to drop you
thirteen stories

the man finishes his glass of water chlorinated water
up state piped down new york water
tense silence and the rosé looks frozen
with the woman's pink lipstick on the crystal rim

yes the boy hadn't remembered the incident
just sits

the hands of a boy who has just been told of his doom
don't tremble
only the woman's hands tremble and it is the privilege of
her role to tremble no matter how pink her nail polish
all a boy can do is not tremble
stare at the rosé
not look at his father
mother

get up and not really experience what was said
words beginning to rake his memory
yet memory not scarred yet
get up not to feel who screamed then or now
walk
across
the room

my story was played
threethousandfivehundred years ago
it was a patriarch's privilege
lying to his spouse taking the boy on a trip
bound him sharpened his knife to
cut out his youth
after he had waited a lifetime for the child to be born

every scholar knows that story never took place
genesis saga hebrew folk tale
which makes it so much worse
than if it had been history

to live with a few schizoids is our daily bread
but to live
with that story
made up
fictitious revelation about an almost murder

by real almost criminals
sitting around tents and enjoying themselves
boys patriarchs
lying to the women about their cunning plans for slaughter

when elie wiesel came out of auschwitz he
had to write a story
abraham and isaac
if you cease telling the saga you have to live with your crime
abraham and isaac didn't happen
then laugh with me
let the storyteller frighten you
to know with the recall
of bitterness and the colors
of doom laugh laugh
inhuman play with my locked-up lips
wild contrary symbols in the
rhythm of absurd emotions

when i experience abraham's inhumanity
when i feel
the deed of murder and waking up half way
fearful still from dream and nightmare
at times from orgasm and touch and torn lips
from the night that was strong enough
for dawn to rage as the day arose

laughing that men could have the gall to claim
some god told abraham
not to kill
after the boy lay there already
mind you
knowing he was meant to get the knife
how absurd and cruel and inhuman
to have the god say
don't do it
love him
after commanding abraham to take him there

i don't need to excuse abraham
any more
nor isaac
nor forgive

no one told abraham to do it
no one told him not to do it

the celebration mutates
into the soft silent morning

but the curse goes on
many years later united nations had come to new york
and the knifings of cabbies
the boy had grown into success
aristocratic success like his father
human sophisticated warm gifted cunning lonely
like his father i said

once in a while i meet a human being who does not want to
judge me nor convert me nor even see through me
just drink a glass of simple beaujolais over a clean
tablecloth and the beaujolais is all there is between the
two of us not even a story
delicious slightly cooled refreshing light red celebration
grape of burgundy in a crystal
it doesn't have to be expensive crystal
and what there is between us is in that color of the feast
i don't want to go beyond nor let anyone come beyond
the deep red joy between us
for one inch beyond
might kill
the feast

many years later the boy came to his godchild's campus
forty years is a long time to recall
except if you had been in a desert even for forty days
without embrace
you would want to feast for nights
rosé snails châteaubriand médoc
no matter the catharsis

to the campus of his godchild i said one afternoon
proud teenager suffering
not yet strong enough to sustain
life without love
not yet drunk from the bitter
aftertaste of fear
watches the boy's still clumsy motions paralyzed
by his parents' tyranny
and the curse of memory came over him
didn't i say words are insane

don't feel so lousy kid
care to know what they did to me some decades ago
my father hung me one day
he used to wave to my mother with branches of spirea
out of a window
by my left leg
how 'bout that

hell
did he drop
you

it was thirteen stories up
murder kiddo murder and i never forgot it
boy there's murder in your youth and you don't know it

why did the man tell the boy
why did the boy tell the boy

what will the boy do with that information
freeze
and i saw him freeze and felt the acid
images deform the texture of his memory
one day in a moment of rage
when the wine spills on the white tablecloth
and he can't take any longer the pain of being human
what will he do
what will i do with the information
the isaac story ended by some deus telling the old man
not to kill as if absurdity would be easier to take
with a hollywood ending
and future firstborn would be more loved and hence more
loveable but i can't save that boy
and the man is too old and isaac is gone
and the caves of lascaux

i want to terminate the dream
exegete
doubt
make a movie out of that staged sacrifice by
cutting out the ending exchange names
shoot new scenes and play old ones backward
sing a new song to the song of murderers

i shall do to the story
what the story did to the deed

sing a new song to abraham
old fool that you are
to the men who created isaac
old fools in your tents

prime time show isaac killed abraham show
happy ending and a word from our sponsors or

just before abraham was about to tie isaac with a rope
they had a big fight and after the fight they toasted
to their game with bourbon and ginger ale the american way
or shall i say abraham invited isaac to lüchow's for
sauerbraten discussed the matter in good old germanic
fashion by which i mean abraham paid and when isaac didn't
accept the old man's philosophy abe took him out on
broadway and beat him up cut his long hair right under the
electronic headlines on times square and the two read
immediately that they had created history
so isaac paid for the sacrificial lamb saying to abraham
come on man i understand you are in a lot of troubles and
we should never have left the plains of mesopotamia
and abe thought ike was one hell of a kid and they settled
the matter then and there and went to bermuda for a cruise

make isaac say
daddy what's wrong with mother why is she not here
you should be making love to her and not to me
and daddy whacked the dirty brat one
and said you've got a point
went over to lot's wife and looked at her pink nails
and asked her for a kiss

or isaac said
i'm exploited old man and instead of exploiting me
you do the job and work for a while where cain left off
then let me light the fire and watch its
crackling and its death
and abraham said jacob is not born yet
so isaac replied that's the trouble with you marxists
you always think in linear terms

and isaac sent the old man to a psychoanalyst who made
fifty-two appointments with him for forty years
a lot of dough to spend on women man

and then made appointments with the boy and after a while
they made double dates the boy and abraham
provided the psychoanalyst doesn't end in jail because
he makes love to his godchild in the freshman class

and then abraham takes a metroliner down from new york
we pick him up ceremoniously at 30th street station and
wine dine flirt castrate bait him in the carpeted cave
a club four elevator heights above the ghetto
put a tie on him since it would be blasphemy to
feast a mithraic banquet in mere blue jeans
his blue jeans smell but there is no law against that
loves to be feted in the land of smashed schlitz cans and
stripped chevrolets
the clown wouldn't have dared to ask
300 bucks for his reading without his terrific beard
author of pentateuch
enjoys double martinis by which to exalt our exodus
we meander with him up broad street and love
his warm witty laughter and he loves our angst
about to cross the street he trips by mistake isaac
black isaac
dressed up
drop out
laid off
urbanized to give character to authentic poetry readings
in authentic ghetto situations
isaac who bales for historical replay right here on the
cracked concrete get off my feet you white s o b
abrahamic teeth producing that high pitched
damage to ear nerves
blood on the concrete
abraham paid to glorify my violence
didn't exactly enter the land of cain with quaker meetings
which is why isaac runs for his life

that's not in the book and no divine intervention
just a poet wiping blood off his shirt
about twenty minutes later stumbles on the lectern
rhythm of anger sung with the insanity of vengeance
as if pain could ever solve our
futile sacrifices
i bet he doesn't hear one single line of his own
just mine
just feels red streaks of his retina
descend down his battered face to the poorly washed
cut in his beard
i'm not even sure what i'm clapping for
double martinis back in the cave
or my own
fantasies between
his lines

i'm telling the story wrong not abraham we brought down
from the village but isaac yellow scarfed at neck isaac
when we picked him up at 30th street his blue jeans stank
the clown wouldn't have dared to ask 120 bucks for his
reading without that army shirt
poet of pristine
agony wounded by the sound
of his own utopia
riotous lunch in the wine-carpeted club where
icons are
drowned in the darwinistic laughter for christian survival
isaac two double martinis extra dry
meanders across broad street trips
abraham
dressed up
drop out
gin drooling down the black tie
laid off
urbanized to give authentic atmosphere to
poetry readings in authentic ghetto soot
abraham

you white s o b get off my sidewalk
stop messin' up my sidewalk you white sidebitch whitebitch
i'll
i'll
the poet
isaac i mean who looks dazed at the sidewalk colored
with his own blood
why need he come down on a metroliner to read
greenwich village new humane new left radical hopeful
i'll give you twenty more adjectives if you pay me poetry
remember how they finally cheat isaac the blind old
clown
to hand out his future to the wrong one
cuddles sort of in the car driven to the afternoon train
all he can do is stare at the sidewalks
smashed beer bottled
from the land of sky blue waters
as if clinical training were worth anything without
his check
not one damn word of thanks
just spits on the sidewalk
huge ugly sputum

fourthousandandfour
b
c
finally we sit
the two of us
deadlocked in the silence of the blood soaked desert
godforsaken
abraham vomits up the smell of putrified
sacrificial flesh while israeli arabs
plow mutilated corpses into soil

caves of lascaux
don't you worry about killing me
harts bisons male taurus female
don't forgive
the red brown ochre of the fallen leaves
can't forgive the grass
mowed for the winter and i'll make it
perhaps
when i reach the limits of my memory
strong enough to
exchange roles

i'll let you play mine if you
promise never again
to sneer at yours

one more chance to
chase across the bosborus and
fling the criminals over the tarpejan rock
hear them cry for crimes no one committed
at salem where the witch
pays with the burning cross
the final price for our deeds

listen abraham
how about playing
with our faces
unmasked

fourthousandandfour
a
d